D1488973

by

Derek Taylor Kent

Illustrations by **Paul Louis Smith**

www.DerekTaylorKent.com

Whimsical World Enterprises

Los Angeles

For information address:
Derek Taylor Kent Books, PO Box 241442, Los Angeles, CA. 90024
www.DerekTaylorKent.com

Library of Congress Cataloging-in-Publication Data
Kent, Derek Taylor.

Principal Mikey / by Derek Taylor Kent ;
Illustrations by Paul Louis Smith — 1st ed. p. cm. — (Principal Mikey)
Summary: Mikey McKenzie is a natural born problem-solver. The only problem he can't solve is that he's just ten-years-old so nobody takes his ideas seriously. But all of that changes when Mikey is given the opportunity to become principal of his school when kooky Principal Walker gets called away, much to the chagrin of the stern Vice Principal Sherman. Will the school fall apart in a week, or could he possibly make it the best school ever?

ISBN 978-0-9995554-2-2 (Hardcover bdg.)

School—Fiction. 2. Humor—Fiction. 3. Education—Fiction. 4. Humorous St ories.) I. Smith, Paul Louis.,
III. II. Title.

For my beautiful wife, Sheri Kent,
and all our adventures to come.

Contents

PRINCIPAL MIKEY

1

Mikey McKenzie didn't see the world the way any other kid saw it.

When he looked at his surroundings, he didn't accept that things are the way they are and it was his job to adapt to it. Instead, he saw everything that could be better. He saw every ounce of unfairness, every hint of injustice, every drop of waste and every portion of potential.

Simply put, Mikey McKenzie was a natural born problem-solver.

Unfortunately, the only problem he *couldn't* solve was that he was just ten years old and not a single adult took anything he said seriously.

Take for instance, *Operation Squirrel Circus*.

At the intersection of Walnut and Pine Street, just one block away from Mikey's house, the rate of car accidents was six hundred percent higher than any other intersection in town. Mikey didn't know that exact statistic, but what he did know was that he heard the familiar sound of screeching and one car smacking into another car at an average of two-point-seven accidents per week.

Despite Mikey's pleas to the local police, nobody was interested in devoting time to investigate the problem.

So, Mikey decided to conduct his own investigation. He stayed in and finished all of his homework on Friday night so that he would have the entire weekend free to focus on this mystery.

Saturday morning he planted himself at the corner of Walnut and Pine. He brought a lawn chair, a bag of chips, a peanut butter sandwich, a pair of binoculars, and a notepad for writing his observations.

For three hours, he sat and watched the traffic go by. The streets were busy with people heading out to their brunches or to the park, but there wasn't a single fender-bender—not even a sudden stop the entire day.

How strange, Mikey thought to himself, while he doodled the surroundings on his notepad. He concluded that his presence had somehow caused an environmental shift that was preventing an accident from occurring. However, he had no idea why.

Mikey raised his binoculars toward Walnut Street. It was called Walnut Street because it was lined with robust, leafy walnut trees that draped over the sidewalk and curb.

The trees were virtually empty. Mikey thought that was strange since walnut trees are usually occupied by squirrels feasting on their bounty.

Mikey turned his attention to Pine Street. It was called Pine Street because it was lined with majestic pine trees that towered over their stouter walnut neighbors.

When Mikey scanned the pine trees with his binoculars, one mystery was solved. There were scores of squirrels in the trees looking directly at him. Shocked, he nearly choked on a potato chip.

Why were all the squirrels leaning on the edges of the branches, staring at him as if he were a bear planning to climb up the tree to eat them?

That's when Mikey realized what was going on. The squirrels thought that any creature patiently sitting in between them and their food source must be a predator waiting for them to venture down. They didn't want to get gobbled up, of course.

Mikey didn't think he looked like a scary predator at all. He had short black hair that hung uneventfully over his forehead like a thin layer of chocolate frosting over a vanilla cupcake. The kind that when you get one you think, *Hey!*

Where's all the frosting?

On top of that, he had a spindly but agile body, not unlike a squirrel's. He wore incredibly thick glasses with a heavy black frame, which was necessary to hold the twenty-two layers of lenses. Yes, Mikey was born with one of the worst pair of eyes in human history. Mikey's mother told him she felt terribly guilty that perhaps it was because she didn't eat enough carrots when Mikey was in her tummy, but the doctors assured her it was a genetic fluke.

The only bright side of the situation was that Mikey's eyes had actually improved as he aged. At three years old, he started off with twenty-nine layers of lenses. Each time he went in for his eye exam, his vision had improved enough that the doctors removed one layer from his glasses.

The optometrists assured Mikey's mother that this was also a genetic fluke. Mikey attributed it to the fact that his favorite dessert was carrot cake.

When Mikey realized that his presence had indeed caused an environmental shift, he rushed back home and put on a camouflage outfit. He then ran back to the intersection and hid behind the bushes across the street.

Sure enough, when the hungry squirrels were confident that the coast was clear, they scampered down the pine trees then dashed across the street to the walnut trees.

For the rest of the afternoon, Mikey watched the squirrels munch the walnuts and chase each other across the branches. As the sun began to set, it was time for the squirrels to hit the hay, or hit the twigs in their case. They dashed across the street to their pine tree homes. After some quick research, Mikey learned squirrels did this because trees can get quickly infested with bugs, birds, or parasites, so they often have to move from tree to tree.

Just as Mikey suspected, when the first squirrel tried to cross the street, a car screeched to a halt in front of it. The car traveling behind it also came to a sudden stop, avoiding a fender-bender by mere inches.

Certain he had solved the case, Mikey rushed over to the police station and told them what he had seen, proudly showing them his detailed notes.

The policemen thought he was awful cute, but unfortunately, they didn't take him seriously (as was often the case). They told him they'd look into it, but when Mikey heard them burst out laughing as soon as he left, he knew they probably weren't going to do anything about it.

When nothing changed after a week, Mikey realized it was up to him to solve the problem. And thus, *Operation Squirrel Circus* went into effect.

Mikey found about fifty feet of thick rope and researched how to form a lasso. He hurled the rope like an expert cowboy onto the top branches of the squirrels' pine tree.

Next, he took the other end of the rope and climbed the walnut tree across the street. He tied the rope into a tight knot around its thick trunk. Now the squirrels had a suspension highway to reach their food source and no longer had to cut across the dangerous intersection.

Sure enough, the squirrels took to their new rope bridge right away. Like furry little tightrope walkers, dozens of squirrels scampered across to the walnut trees for their breakfast. Unfortunately, the daredevil squirrels were such a peculiar sight, several motorists became distracted, ran the stop sign, and got into an accident. But after the first few days, drivers got used to the spectacle and Mikey closed the case on *Operation Squirrel Circus*.

However, solving squirrel mysteries was a piece of cake compared to the problems he would soon encounter. What you are about to read is the story of how Mikey became the first and only kid in the history of the world to become principal of his school.

Most kids wouldn't take that job for a million bucks. After all, who would want that kind of responsibility, or for their classmates to be scared of them? Mikey thought it would be worth it because he truly believed that school could be the type of place that when you wake up in the morning, you're as excited to go there as a trip to Disneyland.

But, as I said, we'll get to that. For now, back at home, Mikey had another problem to deal with. Namely, his big sister, Tracy.

2

"Ughgh, you're sooo annoying!" Tracy bellowed at Mikey. She snatched back her cell phone that he had playfully pocketed, then shoved him out of her room.

"And stay out!" Tracy barked, slamming the door in Mikey's face. Frustrated, Mikey pressed his ear to the door to eavesdrop on her conversation.

"You better not be listening at the door, Mikey, or I'm telling Mom!"

Mikey grimaced. He wanted to continue the game with her and remain lurker at her door, or perhaps knock on it loudly then run away to get her *really* mad, but it didn't seem like Tracy was in the mood to play games. In fact, she was never in the mood to play games with him anymore.

Tracy had turned twelve only six months ago. In that time, Mikey felt like he was living with a brand-new person who had somehow taken control of his sister's body.

Less than a year ago, Tracy would have staked out the corner of Walnut and Pine with Mikey all weekend. She would have taken diligent notes as her brother reported the squirrel's behavior.

Those days seemed like a distant memory.

Mikey could remember the exact moment when everything changed. It was a warm Sunday in July. Mikey was pushing Tracy on the park swing set. They were both laughing and having a great time.

She whipped her long brown ponytail and kicked outward, sending herself higher on the upswing. Her toes scraped the sand each time she came swinging back.

Two of Tracy's classmates, Katie and Skyler, walked by and took notice of them. When Tracy saw the girls, she got off the swing, sat on the park bench and pulled out her ponytail, acting as if she were babysitting Mikey.

"Why are you always hanging out with your brother?" Katie asked.

"Yeah, he's weird," Skyler added.

Mikey almost pitied those two girls. He waited for Tracy

to march over and knock their blocks off for insulting him. But instead, Tracy replied, "Oh, um, I'm just bored, I guess."

"We're going to the mall," Katie announced. "Want to come with?"

"Yeah! Sure!" Tracy chirped with excitement. She joined her friends, leaving Mikey alone at the swings without even saying goodbye.

Mikey stormed back home, crying. He told his mom that Tracy had ditched him at the park. His mom explained that Tracy was at an age when hanging out with her brother just wasn't cool anymore. That didn't make Mikey feel better. He took it that Tracy didn't think *he* was cool enough anymore. The thought made Mikey furious. How could *she* be cooler than him? They played the same video games, they watched the same TV shows, they even went to the same science camp last summer! If anything, neither of them were cool at all!

Mikey decided he had a new mission. He was going to prove to Tracy that he was still cool enough to hang out with. Then she would play with him again instead of talking on the phone or going to the mall with her stupid friends.

Unfortunately, Tracy wasn't Mikey's only problem around the house. Three months before, Mikey's parents had read an article in a parenting magazine that said excessive TV and video games are bad for a child's development. Whatever that meant, it boiled down to Mikey only being allowed one hour of TV or video games a day. Even on weekends.

It was totally unfair.

Mikey's best friend, Justin, got to play Xbox or iPad games as much as he wanted after his homework was finished. Mikey used to compete with him to see who could beat new games the fastest. But because of his parents' lat-est rules, Mikey was way behind on all of them. He had re-cently stopped talking to Justin about games because what-ever stage Mikey was at was always old news.

To make matters worse, the same article said that kids should have at least two after-school activities. So, Mikey's parents signed him up for soccer. When the coach told Mikey's parents that at ten years old, he lacked the agility of most two-year-olds, instead of taking him out of soccer, they immediately signed him up for his second after-school activity—ballet. You know, to improve his agility.

Mikey was even worse at ballet than he was at soccer. Now he spent his after-school time doing two things he hat-ed, which made him feel completely helpless.

Mikey tried to tell his parents that he would much rath-er join a nature club that went on hikes or volunteer at the local zoo, but again, Mikey was only ten years old. Even though his parents *physically* heard the words he had said, they didn't really listen to him and did not take his request seriously.

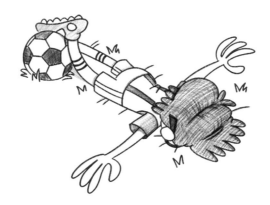

What is it with parents always thinking they know best?

As Mikey lay awake in his bed at 9:52 p.m. on a Sunday night in mid-October, it dawned on him that all the rules and restrictions placed upon him were slowly, but surely, ruining his life.

The sheer number of problems in his life weighed upon him like a blanket made out of heavy chains. The worst part was that for the first time, Mikey couldn't think of a solution to any of his problems that didn't involve him magically aging eight years overnight. He dreamed of a day when people would treat him like an adult.

Little did he know that the following Monday would be the day that everything changed.

3

Monday

Prairie View School was the only option in town for every third- through eighth-grader. Had there been another choice, every kid at school would have chosen to attend a different school.

The main reason was the new vice principal, Mr. Sherman. Principal Walker had recently hired Mr. Sherman to be in charge of discipline. To say he was strict would be the understatement of the year. He wore the same brown suit every day that matched his neatly combed brown hair. The rumor was that Mr. Sherman used to be a drill sergeant in the marines, and nobody doubted it.

The first thing Mr. Sherman did was to ban gum chewing at school. Jeremy Ramer tested that rule when he tried to sneakily chew some bubble gum behind the gym bleachers during lunch. Unbeknownst to him, Mr. Sherman was lurking in the rafters beneath the ceiling. He slid down a pole and caught Jeremy mid-chew. Jeremy was issued a week's detention with yard cleanup duty.

Jeremy wasn't alone as dozens of other kids joined him who had never been caught rule-breaking before. It was like Mr. Sherman had ESP for mischief.

Even though Mr. Sherman was a big problem for many kids, Mikey didn't like to concern himself with problems he knew he couldn't solve. He figured that if the new vice principal didn't want anyone to break the rules, then the easiest solution was not to break the rules. Case closed.

There were several other reasons why kids at Prairie View would have preferred a different school. The campus was dirty, the computers were ancient, the lunches were gross and smelly, and the sports teams stunk even worse. A major reason the sports teams hardly ever won was because bullies ruled the sports fields on the playground, so even the best athletes were too afraid to practice. Due to the greasy food and lack of exercise, the majority of students were not in the best of shape and the school and parents blamed each other. But all of these concerns vanished the instant Mikey stepped into his classroom that Monday morning and halted in shock.

He had to wipe off the twenty-two lenses on his glasses to make sure he wasn't seeing things. Half the class was missing. Normally, you'd expect a few kids, at most, to be out sick on any given day, but half the class? Was today a holiday he didn't know about?

Mikey sat next to Justin. He always sat beside his best friend in class because they could jabber about things like computers and science for hours on end. Justin was more than a bit on the chunky side and his wavy light brown hair seemed to defy gravity by growing upward, which always made him look like he had bed-head.

"Hey, where is everybody?" Mikey asked Justin.

Justin replied, "Mrs. Hughes said that half the class is home with the flu. She just got called into an emergency meeting with Principal Walker."

"Half the class is gone? This is crazy!"

Mikey was very glad Justin wasn't out sick. If he were, the class bullies would seize the opportunity to trip Mikey in the hallway or play keep-away with his glasses during recess. Then they'd fall over laughing when Mikey ran into a tree.

Because he was one of the big kids in class, Justin protected Mikey from being picked on too much.

Justin continued, "It's not just half the class. It's half the school."

"Half the school? We must have gotten lucky."

"I wouldn't call it luck, good friend. Since we stick to ourselves and don't socialize with the other kids, we probably weren't exposed to the same germs. Our anti-social tendencies may have saved our lives. Or at least a few days of puking."

That's another reason Mikey liked Justin. He was great at generating a hypothesis, which is an educated first guess as to the reason for a mysterious event. They made a great team because once Justin formed a hypothesis, Mikey would take over and devise a plan to either prove or disprove it.

Justin guessed that he and Mikey had avoided illness because they tended to isolate themselves from the other kids. True enough, but they were still in close proximity during most classes. If the flu was highly contagious, why weren't all of the kids out sick?

Mikey began to devise a plan to figure out the reason for the baffling illness. If he could solve this one mystery, maybe adults would take him seriously. Like any of his operations, the first step would be observation and data collection.

Operation Virus Eradication was under way.

The classroom door flew open and Mrs. Hughes entered wearing a blue surgical mask. She announced, "Principal Walker ordered us to wear these surgical masks so that none of you spread your germs to the teachers. A great idea, I say. A nasty flu at my age could earn me a one-way ticket to the hospital."

Mrs. Hughes was a very good teacher, but also a little wacky. She always wore gloves and walked around with an umbrella to block the sun. If it rained, she would put her umbrella away and let herself get wet because the sun wasn't out. She looked like she could be a young grandma as she still had most of the color in her black hair, but may have been older as she kept very good care of her pale complexion. She bragged that not a single sunray had touched her face in ten years.

Despite her nuttiness, Mrs. Hughes was a great teacher because she was genuinely excited about every subject she taught. Her enthusiasm spread like a ... well ... like a wonderfully infectious disease to all the students, who consequently loved to learn from her just as much as she loved to teach.

Mrs. Hughes walked across the room and sprayed a disinfectant above all of the kids' heads.

"Try not to breathe in too deeply," Mrs. Hughes said sweetly, spraying the mist and tightening the mask across her face.

Justin

Mikey raised his hand and asked, "Mrs. Hughes, are any of the teachers also out sick?"

"No," she said. "All of the teachers are present. Why do you ask?"

"No reason," said Mikey.

Mrs. Hughes smirked. She knew that Mikey was up to something. Ever since she had taught Mikey the scientific method of establishing hypotheses, gathering evidence, and creating a theory, it had jumpstarted his determination to unravel all the world's mysteries. She was proud of him, but also worried his curiosity could land him into trouble.

Mikey took out a pad and wrote down the first clue: *No teachers affected.* His first thought was that the sickness must have originated from a place that the kids share but where teachers don't go. Mikey looked around the room. It was a mixture of boys and girls. Mikey wrote down a second clue: *Most likely not from a boys' or girls' bathroom as both boys and girls are out sick in equal numbers.*

Mikey passed the note to Justin. Justin read the clues. With a mutual nod, *Operation Virus Eradication* was in motion.

Principal Walker's voice crackled over the school PA system. "Attention, students and faculty. I have just found out that I will have to leave the school for the next couple weeks for personal business. Starting tomorrow, Vice Principal Sherman will be the acting principal of the school until I return. I have full faith that he will be able to handle this terrifying epidemic. Remember, always use a tissue when you sneeze, and wash your hands if you touch anything that might have a germ on it. Toot-a-loo!"

Mikey and Justin looked at one another and gulped. When the class realized that Principal Walker's words were no joke, that Mr. Sherman was about to become the principal, every student shouted, "Nooooo!"

4

Mikey noticed that his classmates could hardly concentrate on their work after the announcement that Mr. Sherman was taking over as principal. It was nearly everyone's worst nightmare come to life.

Mikey tried to put thought of Mr. Sherman out of his head. As far as he was concerned, Mr. Sherman being in charge was a problem he couldn't solve. He preferred to focus on the problems he *could* solve.

As soon as the recess bell rang, Mikey and Justin ran to the schoolyard to begin their investigation for *Operation Virus Eradication*.

During the fractions lesson, Justin had formed a new hypothesis that the source of the contamination was likely a popular piece of playground equipment. Since the teachers didn't use the playground equipment, it would explain why none of them were out sick.

The duo roamed around the schoolyard, observing the activity. The teachers on yard duty wore white paper masks over their noses and mouths while they watched the kids at play. The masked teachers looked super creepy, but Principal Walker didn't want half the faculty getting sick as well.

Mikey and Justin whipped out their pencils and pads. They took detailed notes on which students were using which piece of equipment.

Only the girls were at the hopscotch courts. That area was eliminated. Only boys were on the basketball court, so that was eliminated as well.

The one piece of equipment that seemed to have an

equal number of girls and boys was the merry-go-round.

The girls sat in the center of the spinning disc. The boys stood on the outside and held onto the outer bars to spin it as fast as they could. The girls screamed with delight as the platform spun faster and faster until they couldn't take it anymore. Then the boys abruptly stopped the spinning. The girls stepped off, walking around dizzily until they fell over onto the sand. It was apparently a contest to see who could stand up the longest before falling over.

Once the girls recovered, the boys sat on the merry-go-round and the process was repeated. A longhaired kid named Stanley Roberts managed to stay upright the longest, but then he threw up all over the ground.

When he finished, he shouted, "Whoooa. Totally awesome! That was the best ride yet!"

"That must be it!" declared Justin. "An equal number of girls and boys used the merry-go-round. While they were spinning, I noticed that the wind was causing drool to fly out of their mouths onto the face of whoever was sitting next to them."

"I think you're right," said Mikey. "Plus, that vomit must be filled with germs."

"Am I the hypothesis master or what?" Justin said, proudly.

"You are the master. Let's collect samples so we can prove our theory."

Mikey and Justin slapped on rubber gloves. They took out their tools for sample collection—swabs, petri dishes, cotton swabs, a spoon, and plastic baggies.

As soon as there was an opening, Mikey and Justin jumped onto the merry-go-round. They swabbed the bars and the platform. They collected tiny globules of spit in the petri dish. They even held their noses, scooped up a sample of Stanley's vomit, and dropped it into the plastic baggie.

The students were looking at Mikey and Justin like they were nuts, but they were already considered the weird kids, so they were used to it.

Once the samples were collected, they rushed back to the science lab. As they were running, they heard the loud voice of Mr. Sherman bark at them, "NO RUNNING IN THE HALLWAY!"

Mikey and Justin froze on the spot.

"Sorry, Mr. Sherman," said Mikey. "I didn't mean to—

Mikey stopped speaking when he saw his sister, Tracy, walking next to Mr. Sherman, crying.

"Tracy, what's wrong?" Mikey asked.

Before Tracy could answer, Mr. Sherman barked, "Attention! All of you!"

Every kid in the hallway froze in place and stared at Mr. Sherman and Tracy.

"I caught this girl stealing makeup from another girl's locker. There is zero tolerance for thievery. Let this be a lesson to all of you!"

"But, Mr. Sherman," Mikey pleaded, "Tracy is my sister. She's never stolen anything in her life. It must be a mistake."

"No mistake," said Mr. Sherman. "I saw her with my own

eyes." He marched Tracy to his office.

Mikey felt bad for Tracy, but if she really had stolen something, detention would serve her right.

A few minutes before lunch ended, Justin and Mikey found Mrs. Hughes. They convinced her to let them borrow one of the school's high-powered microscopes.

Justin placed the first petri dish under the lens and looked into the eyepiece.

"What do you see?" asked Mikey, hopping up and down with excitement.

"I see ... nothing. No viruses or bacteria."

Disappointed, Mikey stopped jumping. They continued examining the samples, but could find no evidence of any harmful microscopic entity.

Plugging their noses, they put some of Stanley's vomit on the glass slide and took a gander. Although it was totally gross (and cool) to see magnified digested food and stomach acid, there was no evidence of a flu virus.

"How strange," said Justin, dejected. "I guess my hypothesis was incorrect."

The end-of-recess bell rang. Justin and Mikey could hardly focus the rest of the morning. They racked their brains for another way the virus could be spreading.

At the end of lunch, they returned back to Mrs. Hughes' class with their heads hung in defeat. Then, they noticed a line of kids that stretched down the hallway.

Stanley Roberts stood at the end of the line. They asked him what the line was for. Stanley, still dizzy from a recent ride on the merry-go-round said woozily, "Ohhh duuudes, the little kids' drinking fountain broke last week. Now they have to share with us. Even the third graders can barely reach the faucet."

Mikey and Justin both looked at each other with excitement.

"It makes perfect sense," Justin said to Mikey. "An equal number of boys and girls use the drinking fountain."

"Plus, the kindergartners, first and second-graders are the germ-iest kids in the school. Of course they would be spreading it to the others," Mikey added.

"Plus, none of the teachers use this fountain. That explains why they're not sick!"

Mikey and Justin rushed to the front of the line where Stanley's story was confirmed. The younger, shorter kids stood on their tippy-toes, but couldn't quite reach their mouths high enough to gulp the water, so they slobbered all over the faucet instead.

"Gross!" Mikey and Justin said together.

After several little kids had taken their drinks, Mikey and Justin cut into the line. They took their samples as the other kids angrily hollered at them. A couple of sixth-graders really wanted to sock Mikey, but Justin shot them a look and they backed off.

They rushed back to the empty classroom and observed the new samples under the microscope. Sure enough, there were hundreds of flu viruses having a big party in the petri dish. They looked like tiny golf balls with sharp spikes bouncing off one another.

Mikey and Justin high-fived. *Operation Virus Eradication* was now a theory supported by evidence.

Mrs. Hughes walked into the room and raised her eyebrows at the boys' ridiculous celebratory dance.

"Ahem," she said. "What are you two so happy about?"

"We found the origin of the flu epidemic!" exclaimed Mikey. "We have to show this to Principal Walker right away."

Unfortunately, as nice as Mrs. Hughes was, she was also one of the adults in the world who took nothing ten-year-olds said seriously. She rolled her eyes and remarked, "Yes, yes, I'm suuuure you did. I hope you two had fun playing scientist, but it's time to take your seats for class."

"But, Mrs. Hughes," Mikey interrupted, "It's true! I promise. You have to let us show our findings to the principal."

That's when the bell rang and the rest of the students shuffled into class.

Mikey continued to prod Mrs. Hughes and tug at her blouse until she turned around sharply and said, "Mr. McKenzie, take your seat this instant. Principal Walker is very busy dealing with a serious health crisis. The last thing she needs is a student barging into her office and making her sick!"

Justin shrugged his shoulders and took his seat, appearing to give up. Mikey guessed Justin didn't care about the discovery being announced. For him, the fun was always in the process. Just knowing they'd succeeded was enough.

But it wasn't enough for Mikey.

Biting his tongue, Mikey took his seat as well. It looked like there was only one way he was going to get to see the principal. He hadn't gotten so much as a detention all year, but that was about to change.

Mrs. Hughes began the Spanish lesson. "One of the most common phrases you will have to know is *Donde esta el baño*? Which means, where is the bath—

"Pffththththth!"

Mikey put his hand to his mouth and made the loud farting noise at the perfect moment. The class erupted in laughter.

"Who did that?" Mrs. Hughes said, angrily.

"I did!" said Mikey, raising his hand.

The students' jaws dropped. No kid had ever admitted so quickly to misbehaving.

Justin was confused at first, but then realized what Mikey was up to. He gave him a thumbs-up.

"Mikey?" said Mrs. Hughes, perplexed. "That's not like you at all. I suppose I'll let this one slide. But one more outburst, and you're in big trouble."

Mikey rolled his eyes. *Great, here we go again*, he thought to himself.

"As I was saying," Mrs. Hughes continued, "the phrase means—

"Teacher is a stinker! Teacher is a stinker!" Mikey chanted.

"That's it, Señor McKenzie! You go straight to Vice Principal Sherman's office!"

"Si, Señora Hughes!"

Mikey quickly gathered his backpack and bolted out of the classroom before Mrs. Hughes could change her mind. When Mrs. Hughes realized that Mikey had tricked her, she shouted, "Hey, wait!"

But it was too late. Mikey was already rounding the corridor to the vice principal's office. Even though Vice Principal Sherman was strict, Mikey was certain he would take his findings seriously for the sake of the school's health.

This was the best Monday he'd had in a long time.

5

Mikey stepped into Vice Principal Sherman's office practically walking on air. He couldn't wait to present the evidence to him. He didn't care if he got a month's detention for insulting the teacher.

However, when he opened the door, he saw the last thing he expected. His parents.

Mikey had inherited their father's thin black hair while his sister had gotten their mother's fuller light brown hair. They were slumped over and looked despondent.

"Mom? Dad? What are you doing here?"

Before they could answer, Principal Walker's door opened. She stepped into the room with Vice Principal Sherman and Mikey's sister. Everyone was strangely quiet.

"Sis, what happened?"

"As if you don't know!" Tracy snapped back. "Are you here to laugh at me?"

"No! Did you get suspended?"

"Suspended? I wish. I just got expelled!"

Tracy ran out of the room, sobbing. Mikey's parents took off after her.

"You expelled her?" Mikey asked Principal Walker, unable to contain his shock.

Principal Walker nodded sadly. Mr. Sherman nodded with pride.

The vice principal added, "It was regrettable, but it was necessary to make an example of her to prevent thefts in the future. What are you doing here? Shouldn't you be in class, Mr. McKenzie?"

"I was… but Mrs. Hughes sent me here."

"Ah, I see mischief runs in the family," Mr. Sherman sneered. "What did you do? Steal an eraser?"

"An eraser? I have my own laptop. I haven't even used an eraser since I was six. But that's not important. I have great news. I know what's making all the kids sick!"

"I'm sure you do, *Dr.* McKenzie," Mr. Sherman muttered, sarcastically. "Don't worry, Principal Walker. I'll handle this one. Step into my office, young man."

Principal Walker just stood there, not sure whether she should intervene. She was very nice, but hated doling out discipline. That's why she had to hire a vice principal. With some jobs, there's such a thing as being too nice.

Mikey decided to give it one last shot. "Please, you have to believe me, Principal Walker. I have the proof right here."

Mikey poured the contents of his backpack onto the floor. "I can show you. If you just look at—

"Enough, Mr. McKenzie! Principal Walker is far too busy to listen to your ridiculous—

"Actually, Carl," said Principal Walker, cutting him off. "I think I can spare a few minutes for Mikey. Why don't you come into my office?"

"But Principal Walker," Mr. Sherman fumed. "It's my job to—

"I said I have this one, Carl. I'll let you know if you're needed."

Mr. Sherman snorted, but reluctantly obeyed. "Of course, Principal Walker. As you wish." He exited into his office and shut the door.

"Come right in," Principal Walker said, smiling. "Show me what you found."

For the next five minutes, Principal Walker listened

as Mikey explained how he and Justin had discovered the origin of the flu virus. She marveled at Mikey's ingenuity and seemed to take him seriously. But then again, Principal Walker was considered to be kind of kooky. She always wore vividly-colored, flowing dresses to school. Her hair often looked liked she had just arrived from a rock concert and she loved playing with kid toys like scooters and yo-yos.

When Mikey finished his presentation, Principal Walker was quiet for a moment, then said, "Let me get this straight. You called your teacher a stinker just so you would get sent to my office to show me *this?*"

"Um … yes."

"Well, young man, that's very, very … *brilliant* of you. Your evidence is quite persuasive. I'm going to have that drinking fountain sanitized immediately. A stool will be placed in front of it so the smaller children won't have trouble."

"Really? You're actually taking my suggestion?"

"Of course. I don't see why not. In fact, I'm going to make an announcement right now."

Principal Walker pushed a red button on her desk. Her voice sounded throughout the school's PA system. "Attention, teachers and students. A very smart student named Mikey McKenzie has discovered the origin of the flu epidemic. I am happy to report that in mere minutes, all of us shall be safe. Teachers, you are free to remove your surgical masks. This is Principal Walker saying good—"

"Wait!" said Mikey, leaping onto her desk and speaking into the microphone. "Justin Gluck also helped!"

Unfortunately, the classes didn't hear Mikey credit Justin as the principal had taken her finger off the button. Principal Walker gave Mikey a disapproving look, but shrugged it off.

"So, Mr. McKenzie, any other bright ideas before I send you back to class?"

Mikey's heart leapt like a horse bursting out of the gates. He realized this could be his one chance to have the principal's undivided attention. Not only that, she might actually act on his suggestions. Mikey launched into a speech that covered all the school's problems and how they could be fixed.

Mikey began with his idea of how to solve the obesity problem, simply by adding five minutes onto lunch. At first Principal Walker was confused. She thought more lunch time would simply lead to more eating. Mikey explained that most kids would spend the extra time playing, which would burn about fifty calories over those five minutes. Over the course of a week, that's two hundred fifty calories. Over the forty-week school year, that would be ten thousand calories! Kids would lose an average of three pounds they would have otherwise gained, which is like fifteen adult pounds!

"Wow," said Principal Walker. "That just might solve the problem of Prairie View finishing dead last in the state on every physical fitness test." Then she leaned in and whispered, "We don't tell you students that so you don't feel bad about yourselves."

Emboldened by the principal's praise, Mikey next explained that they could improve test scores by installing a reward-based system for success as opposed to a punishment-based system for failure. Mikey thought this would work because he used to get a time-out whenever he didn't do his chores. Oftentimes he chose to not do his chores and take the time-out. However, when his parents installed an allowance-based system where he earned money for each chore, Mikey never missed a chance to do the dishes or sort the laundry. He believed the same principle could be applied to homework, test-taking, and even behavior.

As Principal Walker listened to him explain his ideas, she sat back in awe. "Have you ever thought about becoming a school principal?" she asked him.

"Yeah, right," said Mikey. "And have every kid be scared of me? No, thank you. Me and Justin are going to start our own video game company and be millionaires before we graduate high school."

Principal Walker laughed. "I have no doubt. I will certainly take all of your suggestions into consideration. Now, I think it's time that you got back to class."

His heart still racing, Mikey collected himself and said, "Thank you for your time," and he headed toward the door, feeling fantastic. But then he remembered what had just happened to his sister. His mood shifted to gloomy. It's really weird when something terrible and something wonderful both happen within five minutes of one another.

As Mikey left Principal Walker's office, he turned and saw a very kooky expression on her face, as if she were in the middle of a very kooky thought.

Mikey brushed it off since she was a very kooky principal, but he had a feeling there was a very kooky plan at work in her very kooky brain.

6

After another blooper-fueled soccer practice during which Mikey had played goalie and allowed seven goals in three minutes, he rushed back home to for an update on the day's events. He had been distracted thinking about his sister's expulsion from school, plus coach wouldn't let him wear his glasses so he was basically blind.

Standing at his sister's door, he heard sniffling from inside. He knocked twice. "It's me. Can I come in?"

To his surprise, she replied, "Okay."

He couldn't remember the last time he had been in her room without sneaking in.

Tracy sat on her bed, holding her pet hamster, Princess. Mikey tried to look as sad as he could. He didn't want her to think he was there to make fun of her.

"What happened?" Mikey asked. "Did you really steal something?"

Tracy nodded.

"Why?"

"It wasn't my idea. Skyler and Katie said that if I wanted to be their friend, I had to bring them Melissa Felton's makeup. I knew Melissa's locker combination from when I brought her books when she was out sick. I took some of her makeup while she was outside at recess. Mr. Sherman caught me. He asked what I was doing and I said Melissa said it was okay for me to take it. He called Melissa over. When she said I didn't have permission, I got in trouble for stealing *and* lying."

"Did you tell them it was Skyler and Katie's idea?"

"No! I'm not a snitch. I wouldn't be in any less trouble."

"I know, but you would never have done it if they didn't make you. They should be in trouble, too."

"Shut up! Don't you dare tell anyone! Mom and Dad said there's still a chance we can appeal the decision and get me back in school. If I snitch on them, they'll *never* be friends with me."

Tracy was so mad, it looked like she might throw Princess across the room. Then she settled down, gave Princess a kiss on the head, and put her back in her terrarium.

"You still want to be friends with them?"

"Ugh, you don't understand. It's called hazing. Whenever you join a group, you have to do stupid stuff before they let you in."

"That's dumb. Who would want to join a group like that?"

"You're so immature, Mikey. You just don't get it."

"Well, on the bright side, at least you won't have to go to school for a while, right?"

"I wish. Mom and Dad already found a tutor to home-school me. Unless we move to a new town, I'm going to have to be home-schooled until high school."

"That doesn't sound so bad."

"Yeah, except I won't get to do cheerleading or see my friends during the day. It's going to be boring."

Inside her habitat, Princess started running on the hamster wheel. Mikey and Tracy both studied her, amused at how she never got tired of running in circles.

Tracy wiped away a tear. "I think I might seriously go crazy if I'm cooped in here for the next two years."

"Hey," said Mikey, scratching Tracy's back to comfort her, "you said there's still a chance they can appeal the decision.

I just made friends with Principal Walker today. Maybe I'll be able to help."

Tracy looked at Mikey in disbelief. "You made friends with the principal?"

"It's a long story. But trust me, if there's a way to get you back in school, I'll find it."

7

Tuesday

Mikey and Justin stood in the hallway five minutes before class with enormous grins on their faces. They watched as kid after kid took their drinks at the new and improved water fountain. It had been sanitized, polished, and there was a stepstool at the base.

Some kids gave them pats on the back. Other kids (who would have preferred a few days off of school) gave them dirty looks and the occasional, "Thanks a lot, Einsteins."

It was kind of bittersweet for Mikey. If Tracy were there, she would have been proud of him. She'd have told all her friends that her brother saved them from getting sick. He might have even been invited to eat lunch at the seventh-grade table.

As Mikey sat down in his homeroom with Mrs. Hughes, he noticed that most of the kids who were out sick the day before were now back.

A girl with long blonde hair came over and said, "You couldn't have figured out the problem a week ago? Being sick over the weekend is the worst!"

At 8:00 a.m., the PA system turned on for Principal Walker's daily announcements.

"Students and faculty," she announced, "please proceed immediately to the gymnasium for a special assembly and take a seat with your class. Except for Mikey McKenzie. Please come to my office first."

The class looked at Mikey and went "ooooh" like he was in big trouble.

Mikey tried to think of something he might have done wrong since yesterday, but couldn't think of anything. Maybe his water fountain plan had failed and kids were still getting sick? Nah, too soon to know that.

As the students made their way to the gym, Mikey stepped into Principal Walker's office. She sported an even more colorful dress than the day before. It looked like a five-year-old had done a finger-painting all over it.

"Good morning, Mikey," she chirped. "Please have a seat. I have to make this fast."

Mikey gulped. Was he about to get expelled just like his sister?

"None of the other teachers know what I'm about to tell you. Not even Vice Principal Sherman. The reason I didn't tell them is because, well, they would probably talk me out of it. But before I go through with it, I'm going to need your approval. So, here goes. Mikey, how would you like to be principal of the school?"

Mikey stared at her blankly for several moments. When he saw she was serious, he replied with the most intelligent thing he could think to say.

"Huh?"

"Oh, don't worry. It wouldn't be on a permanent basis. As you know, I have to go away for a bit, and while I'm gone, I need someone to look after the school. To be frank, your ideas sounded quite promising. I hoped to implement them as soon as possible. So, who better to get things started than you? I'll probably be back in a couple weeks at most. Then you can go back to being a regular student."

"So, will I still have to go to classes if I'm principal?"

"Oh, heavens, no! You'll be *far* too busy. But, I've made arrangements for tutoring so you won't miss out on any of the lessons."

Mikey thought hard for a few moments. He felt a mixture of excitement and fear, but couldn't figure out which he felt more.

"Well, it sounds cool. But, even if I wanted to, there's not a chance that my parents would let me."

"As it happens, I have your parents on speakerphone right now. Mr. and Mrs. McKenzie, are you still there?"

"We're here!" Mikey's parents chimed.

"Mikey seems convinced you won't let him be principal.

I think he needs to hear otherwise from the horse's mouth."

"Son," his dad said, "we were skeptical at first. But Principal Walker assured us that everything would be supervised. Your mom and I talked it over and decided that the decision is yours. Either way, we're okay with it."

Mikey's mom added, "Plus it will look great on your college applications! What other kid can say he was principal of his school?"

"Okay," said Mikey. "I'm not sure yet, but thanks."

"We'll see you later, Mikey," his dad concluded. "We're proud of you."

Principal Walker clicked off the speakerphone. "I must say," she said, "you have very cool parents."

"Trust me, they're not that cool," said Mikey. "Is it okay if I say no? I'm not sure I want everyone in school to like me less than they already do. I mean, nobody likes the school principal. No offense."

"None taken. I completely understand if you refuse the offer. In that case, Vice Principal Sherman will take over as principal."

Mikey winced. Mr. Sherman would probably give an expulsion every day just for passing a note in class. He would be letting down the entire school if he allowed that to happen.

"Between you and me," said Principal Walker leaning in to whisper, "I totally disagree with the decision to expel your sister. If it were up to me, a suspension and an apology would have sufficed. I couldn't overturn the decision because that would make me look soft on school crime to the School Board. I could get expelled myself! But since you don't have to worry about that, I see no reason why you wouldn't be able to reverse your sister's expulsion."

Mikey nearly fell out of his chair. This was his chance to make good on his promise and help his sister get back into school. On the other hand, would it be worth it if he got bullied mercilessly for the rest of his days for daring to take a position of authority over the other kids?

Mikey looked down at his dirty sneakers, then back up at the Principal. "My answer is…"

8

"What?" exclaimed Justin. "She wants to make *you* the principal?"

Mikey and Justin hid in a secluded corner behind the school dumpster during recess. No kids ever went there because the smell of garbage was so nauseating. They didn't mind it as much because they found noxious gasses created by decomposing matter fascinating.

"That's right," said Mikey.

"What did you say?"

"I told her I needed some time to think about it, but I need to let her know before lunch time, cause that's her last chance to make the announcement before she has to leave. I wanted to get your input first. What should I do?"

"What should you do? Duh! You take the job!"

"Easy for you to say. Nobody ever beats you up because you're big. What if they beat me up every day after I'm not principal anymore?"

"Dude, I won't let them lay a finger on you. I don't care if I have to quit school to become your personal bodyguard. This is too good an opportunity to pass up. When someone offers you a chance to be in charge, you say yes!"

"That's good to hear," said Mikey. "Cause I already said yes."

"You what?"

"I wanted to give you the chance to talk me out of it while I could still change my mind. But I just couldn't pass up the opportunity to reverse Tracy's expulsion."

"Dude, that's just the tip of the iceberg. You are going to

make the school so awesome!"

"No," said Mikey. "*We're* going to make this school awesome. Partners?"

Mikey extended his hand and Justin shook it vigorously.

"Partners," replied Justin.

Ten minutes before lunchtime, the Prairie View School gymnasium was filled to capacity. When Mikey walked next to Principal Walker as she approach the podium, he noticed most of the student body giving him dirty looks.

Oh great, they seemed to be thinking. *We're just here to see Mikey McKenzie get some kind of award for solving the virus mystery. What a show-off.*

"Good afternoon, everyone," said Principal Walker. "While I will be across the country taking care of my mother, I have to leave someone in charge of the school as the acting principal."

Vice Principal Sherman smiled proudly from his seat. It was clear that Principal Walker hadn't told him about her change of plans. From his chair behind the podium, he straightened his thin brown tie and patted his short brown hair. He stood up and strolled toward the podium to accept his new role as principal.

"I know I told you yesterday that Vice Principal Sherman would be taking over as principal..."

The students groaned in aggravation. But before Mr. Sherman reached the podium, Principal Walker stuck out her hand and held it right in front of his face.

"*But* ... I have had a change of heart."

The students let out a big sigh of relief.

The smile on Mr. Sherman's face dropped. Embarrassed, he scuttled back to his chair behind the podium.

"As it happens, I had a meeting yesterday with a very

bright young man. He had ideas to improve the school that I wouldn't have thought of in a million years. It got me thinking. Why shouldn't one of you be principal of the school? After all, who knows better than the students what the problems are and how things could be better? So, I'm giving one of you the chance to be principal for the next two weeks with all the same powers that I have. Students and teachers, I would like to introduce you to your new principal … Mr. Mikey McKenzie!"

As Mikey approached the podium, he wasn't sure what kind of reaction he would get. However, he certainly did not receive the uproarious applause he had hoped for. As he gazed toward the crowd of students, a sea of fish stared back at him. The teachers shared the same confused look as the students. Vice Principal Sherman fumed with anger.

There was only one student who cheered—Justin. He was trying to get everyone to join along with him, but no one took the bait.

Mikey lowered the microphone to his mouth. He knew this was his one chance to either win everyone over, or be the most despised kid in the history of the school.

He adjusted his twenty-two-lens-thick glasses, cleared his throat, and searched his thoughts for what the crowd would want to hear from him. His palms became sweaty and his glasses fogged up.

Then, from somewhere deep within, he found the most perfect thing he could possibly say.

"NO MORE HOMEWORK!" Mikey shouted into the microphone.

Like an erupting volcano, every kid leapt from their seats at the same time and cheered.

"Mi-key! Mi-key! Mi-key!" they chanted.

Mikey accepted their love with open arms and he pumped his fists in the air.

His first day as principal was off to a great start.

9

It took several minutes for the celebration to die down. Not even Vice Principal Sherman could restore order. Every student cheered, danced, and jumped around like monkeys as soon as Mikey made homework a thing of the past.

Mikey was ushered out of the gym by Principal Walker so he wouldn't get mobbed. As he followed her back to her office, he realized that he might have just made a big mistake. Principal Walker was probably going to take everything back.

When she shut the door behind her, Mikey immediately begged, "Please, don't fire me, Principal Walker. I don't know what came over me. I didn't mean to say no more homework. I'll tell them I was just kidding."

"Relax, Mikey," Principal Walker said, soothingly. "Have a seat."

Mikey plopped down on the small chair in front of her desk.

"No. Not that seat. *This* is your seat now." Principal Walker pulled out her big black, leather chair for him. Mikey smiled and eased into the comfy seat. His feet didn't even touch the ground.

Principal Walker continued, "What's done is done. If you don't think there should be any homework, then that's your policy, Principal Mikey."

Mikey breathed a big sigh of relief. For a moment, he really thought he'd blown it.

Principal Walker knelt down and looked him in the eye through her purple glasses. "The reason I brought you here is because any second now, a whole gang of teachers is going to be knocking on that door. I'm sure most of them will not be happy with what I've done. No matter what they say, you have to be confident and sure of yourself. Remember, I wouldn't have made you principal unless I was one-hundred-percent sure you could do it."

Just as she said that, there was a loud knock at the door.

"Here we go," Principal Walker said. She exhaled and straightened her colorful dress.

The door opened and Vice Principal Sherman marched inside, followed by nearly every teacher.

"What is the meaning of this?" Mr. Sherman demanded, obviously no less furious than from the assembly.

"I beg your pardon," said Principal Walker, "but I don't believe Principal McKenzie said you could come in."

Mr. Sherman's eyes widened. He shot an angry glance at Mikey, who hadn't gotten out of the principal's chair.

Mikey took this as a cue to display his authority and said, "It's okay, Ms. Walker. I will hear the teachers' concerns."

"How could you?" inquired Mr. Sherman, still ignoring Mikey. "Why would you lie to my face and tell me I'm going to be acting principal and then humiliate me in front of the entire school?"

"I apologize for that, Carl. But it was a last minute decision. There was very little time, and I didn't want to be talked out of it."

"This is an insult!" Mr. Sherman barked at Principal Walker. "Are you trying to tell me you're unhappy with my performance as Vice Principal? Why not just fire me?"

"Because," said ex-principal Walker, "I am not unhappy with your job performance. You have done a fine job disciplining the student body, which was exactly why I hired you. It is my belief that the school needs a fresh perspective while I'm gone. Someone who won't be afraid to try new things. Mikey McKenzie has the freshest ideas I've ever heard. That's my final decision."

"In that case," replied Mr. Sherman, much more calmly, "I have had a discussion with the other teachers. We refuse to work for a child. We will not be coming to work until a proper principal is appointed."

The rest of the teachers nodded their agreement.

"You are free to make that choice," said Principal Walker, "but any of you who refuse to work for Mikey will *not* be hired back when I return. Good luck finding another job."

Mr. Sherman and the rest of the teachers were speechless. They had not expected Principal Walker to call their bluff. They looked at one another, sighed, and seemed to relent.

"Well, in that case," said Mr. Sherman, "perhaps we will continue to work for the sake of the students. But only on a very short-term basis."

"Thank you," said Principal Walker, gathering her personal belongings. "I expect each of you to respect Mr. McKenzie' orders just as you would respect mine. If any of you cause any trouble, Mr. McKenzie has the same authority as me to dismiss you from your jobs. If there are no other questions, I will see all of you again in a couple weeks."

Nobody spoke. Principal Walker walked out the door, nodding to each teacher she passed.

The teachers turned to Mikey for his first orders.

"Okay," said Mikey. "If there are no other questions for me, then please return to your classes after lunch. I'll let you know when I think of some new changes. And remember, none of you are allowed to assign any homework."

The teachers seemed like they wanted to say something, but knowing Mikey could make a snap decision and fire them, they decided not to upset him. Instead, they turned and shuffled to the teacher's lounge.

Vice Principal Sherman was the last one to leave. He looked like he was fighting whether to say what was on his mind. Mikey could see his frustration and enjoyed every minute of it.

"Is there anything else?" Mikey asked Mr. Sherman.

Mr. Sherman huffed, then said through gritted teeth, "I suppose not. I am at your service, Mikey McKenzie."

"*Principal* McKenzie."

"Sorry. *Principal* McKenzie."

Mr. Sherman returned to his office, grumbling under his breath.

Mikey reclined in his big chair, feeling like a king at his throne. Then he thought of something. He ran out the door at fast as he could.

He made it outside just as Principal Walker's car was pulling out of the school driveway. Mikey jumped in front of it.

She rolled down her window and said, "Mikey, what's the matter?"

"I just wanted to say thank you. I hope your mom gets better soon."

Principal Walker smiled warmly, patting Mikey on the cheek. "You know, you're the only one who told me that. Just remember, when I first started, I had no idea what I was doing either. Toot-a-loo!"

10

As Mikey watched Principal Walker drive off, it sank in that this was for real. He started to feel a little queasy. Not only was he now in charge of the whole school, but his biggest supporter was no longer there to stand up for him.

That's when Mikey remembered—he had one other supporter.

Back inside the principal's office, Mikey sat at the big desk and pushed the button to the school's PA system.

"Students and faculty," Mikey said, trying to sound as official as possible, "this is your acting principal, Mikey McKenzie. Principal Walker has left. I have officially taken over for her. So, umm … uhh, what was I going to say?"

Mikey lifted his finger off the red button, hitting himself in the head with his palm. He could hear the echoes of laughter from every classroom. *Dang*, he thought, *I should have written this down.* Then he remembered.

"Sorry about that. As I was saying, Justin Gluck, please report to the principal's office immediately. That's all, folks."

From Mrs. Hughes's Spanish class, Mikey heard the students go, "ooooh" out of habit as if Justin were in big trouble. But when they remembered that the principal was his best friend, the "ooooohs" turned into "Awww, forget it."

When Justin entered the office, Mikey stared at him harshly. "Have a seat, Mr. Gluck. What trouble have you gotten into this time?" Mikey couldn't keep a straight face, though, and started laughing halfway through.

Justin laughed along with him. "This is incredible! Abolishing homework was a stroke of genius. What are you going to do next?"

"You mean, what are *we* going to do. I meant it when I said *we're* going to make this school awesome. I want you to be my right-hand-man. You can't be vice principal since we already have Mr. Sherman. So, how about special assistant to the principal?"

"Does it pay?"

"Uhh, I don't have any money. Tell you what, if they give me a paycheck, I'll split it with you."

"Deal. But I don't know about this 'assistant' business. How about … senior consultant?"

"How about we make it Spanish and call you Señor Consultant?"

"I like that even better."

"All right, then. You are my Señor Consultant."

"*Muy bien.* So, what are we going to do first?"

"I took this job for one reason more than any other."

Mikey picked up the phone and dialed his house. His mom picked up.

"Hello?"

"Hi, Mom. It's Mikey."

"Don't you mean Principal Mikey?" his mom giggled to herself and snorted. So not cool.

"How did you know I took the job?" said Mikey.

"As if there were any doubt. We're so proud of you."

"Thanks, Mom. Could you put Tracy on?"

"She's actually in the middle of a lesson with her tutor. I could have her call you later."

"Actually, it's very important. I need to talk to her right away."

"Okay, one second."

Tracy got on the phone. She still sounded in a foul mood.

"What?" she asked, scornfully.

"Hey, Tracy, did you hear the news?"

"That you're the new principal? Yeah. Forgive me for not doing cartwheels, but *my* life still sucks."

"Not anymore, sis. As acting principal, I hereby repeal your expulsion. You can come back to school."

"What? You can do that?"

"Principal Walker said I have all the same powers she had. That includes the final decision on all disciplinary actions."

"Geez, Mikey. You already sound like a real principal."

"I'm trying my best. So, I expect you back in school right away. Sound good?"

"Yes! I'll be there, Mr. Principal."

"Report to my office first thing. We'll have to run your new punishment by Mr. Sherman. I think a week's detention should be enough."

"Oh, come oooon. Can't I just say I'm sorry?"

"Hey, I don't want it to look like I'm showing *too* much favoritism."

"Fiiine. I'll see you when you get home."

"See ya, Trac'."

"And Mikey..."

"Yeah?"

"Don't tell anyone I said so, but you're the best brother *ever.*"

Mikey smiled wider than he had in months. "Thanks."

When Mikey hung up, Justin nodded.

"A bold move. Good call giving her a week's detention. Lets the students know that you won't tolerate thievery."

"My thought exactly. Wow, I've only been principal for twenty minutes and I've already banned homework and totally saved my sister."

"You're off to a killer start," said Justin, giving Mikey a high-five. "But, I think if we put our minds to it, we can really turn this place around."

"I agree, Señor Consultant. What do we do next?"

11

Justin and Mikey spent the rest of lunch working on *Operation Kids-in-Charge.*

The plan was simple—identify the school's problems, brainstorm solutions, pick the best ones, and implement them. Projected outcome: the students of Prairie View School would wake up just as excited on a Monday morning as if it were a Saturday morning.

But how do you take a place that kids dread going to each day and turn it into a place that's as fun as a carnival? They had a lot of work ahead of them.

They wrote down as many problems as they could think of by going through a standard day chronologically:

- waking up is hard because school starts so early

- first classes are boring and make kids want to go back to sleep

- recess starts too late and kids spend all morning waiting for it

- class time is wasted on dealing with kids misbehaving

- bullies take all the good sports equipment and won't let you play with them if you aren't any good.

And that was just the beginning. It was a very long list. Then Justin noticed an open program on the principal's computer. He clicked on it, and to their surprise, a video was preloaded on the screen. Mikey pressed play and Principal Walker appeared. She was sitting at her desk in the office, having recorded herself on the computer's camera.

"Hi, Mikey," Principal Walker said, cheerfully. "If you're watching this message, that means you've started as principal. I hope everything is going well so far. There are some things you should know. In the top left drawer are the keys to the school."

Mikey opened the drawer. Sure enough, there was a large ring with at least twenty keys on it.

"Those keys open every door on the premises. The maintenance crew should open the school in the morning and lock up at night for you, but should you need it, there it is. Also, I couldn't in good conscience let you become principal and cause you to miss out on all your classwork. As smart as you are, not even you could catch up. So, I've set up *Class Cam*."

A new video popped up on the screen that showed a live streaming image of Mrs. Hughes' classroom. It even had sound. Mikey could see and hear Mrs. Hughes teaching the class about the bones in the human body by projecting slides of a skeleton. He kind of wished he were there for such a cool lesson.

Principal Walker continued, "Everything is being recorded and stored on the security camera system. You're going to have to find time to watch all your lessons over the next couple weeks. You will still have to take any tests that come up. That's all for now."

The screen blinked off, leaving the live stream of the lesson running. Mikey sighed. This was going to be a lot of work running the school and being a student, but he didn't take the job thinking it would be easy.

Mikey and Justin worked through lunch brainstorming ideas. Five minutes before the end of lunch, Justin said, "I have an idea that I think you should put into place right away."

Justin entered the lunch hall first. Because the lunch period was only forty-five minutes, kids usually ate as fast as they could so they had more time to play and socialize. As was the routine, the students cleaned up the lunch area before heading back to their classrooms.

Justin rounded up the students into the lunch hall and proclaimed at the top of his lungs, "May I have your attention, please? Your new principal has a special announcement. I give you, Principal Mikey!"

The kids cheered, still on cloud nine from no longer having any homework. They were hopeful that he would have a new policy as good as that one. The teachers at the faculty table trembled in fear for the same reason.

He climbed on top of a lunch table and basked in his peers' approval. From the corner of his eye, he saw his sister walk into the lunch hall just in time to see him in action.

"Thank you, everybody. It has been an honor to serve you thus far. And don't worry, you still won't have any homework as long as I'm principal."

The lunch hall erupted in more cheers.

"I am hereby extending the lunch period by an extra fifteen minutes. Please enjoy your extra time and use it to have as much fun as you can."

The cheers were so loud, the teachers had to cover their ears.

"In addition, I am also adding fifteen minutes onto P.E. Now you have more time to enjoy the sports you love, and I'm assigning extra teachers to supervise to make sure no bullies will ever steal a ball from you or make fun of you while you play ever again!"

The kids jumped up and clanged the silverware on the lunch trays. This was going very well. Mikey continued, "When you go home tonight, make sure to tell your parents that school now ends at three-thirty instead of three-o'clock."

Nobody objected because the extra time was for activities they enjoyed, and nobody suspected it was a strategic plan to solve the school's obesity problem. The glorious chanting commenced once again: "Mi-key! Mi-key!"

Once again, Mikey got swept away in the moment and felt the familiar impulse from deep inside to make another grand announcement.

"Lastly, I know that there is one thing that we all love to eat more than anything else. So, from now on, there will be pizza for lunch *every day*!"

The cheers were so loud, the teachers ran from the hall to prevent hearing loss.

The cafeteria workers looked confused, but eventually clapped along with the kids. They probably thought that making the same thing every day would definitely make their jobs easier.

"And now," Mikey concluded, "I have to go back to my office to think of more ideas. Rest assured, you can count on lots more great changes as long as I'm principal. Enjoy your lunches."

As Mikey exited the lunch hall, the kids continued chanting, "Mi-key! Mi-key!"

When he passed by Tracy, she gave him a big hug and whispered, "You were awesome," in his ear.

"You really think so?"

"I know so."

Mikey smiled as he walked back to his office with Señor Consultant Justin by his side.

"Really? Pizza every day?" Justin inquired. "According to my calculations, those extra calories will negate the time we added for more exercise. How are they supposed to stay in shape?"

"Oh. I didn't think of that. You think they can make healthy pizzas?"

"Sure. I bet the kids would *love* that," replied Justin sarcastically. "Listen, as your consultant, I have to advise you not to make any more snap decisions without running them by me first. Now we have a big problem on our hands. Pizza every day sounds great at first, but what if they get sick of it?"

Mikey felt really annoyed. Justin had just taken all the steam out of his big moment. Without thinking he blurted, "Fine, *smarty-pants*, why don't you handle this one and let me worry about the bigger problems?"

Noticing the quivering lip on Justin's face, Mikey immediately realized the effect of his words and felt awful. "I'm sorry. I didn't mean it. I'll run things by you from now on, okay?"

Mikey patted him on the back, and Justin looked to feel a little better.

At that moment, Mr. Sherman stormed past them holding Stanley Roberts by the arm.

"What did Stanley do?" Mikey asked.

Mr. Sherman stopped, looking aggravated that he had to explain himself to Mikey. "This boy spilled a tray of food on a teacher by accident, or so he claims. I'm going to write him up for a week of detention."

Mikey didn't believe that Stanley would do such a thing on purpose. He decided to put a stop to Mr. Sherman's punishments right now.

12

Mikey led Mr. Sherman and Stanley into the principal's office.

"I can handle this," said Mr. Sherman to Mikey. "I'm sure you have more important matters to attend to."

"No. Before you hand out any detention time, I want to hear his side of the story. Go ahead, Stanley."

Stanley brushed back his long hair and shifted his eyes back and forth. "Uhhh, yeah, you see, Mikey, I mean, Principal Mikey, I was carrying a tray of food to my table, but there was milk on the floor. I slipped on it and uhhh ... all my spaghetti went flying into Ms. Corning's lap. It was a total accident."

"I understand. Do you have any contradictory evidence, Mr. Sherman?"

"Yes. The boy is a liar. Just today at recess, Ms. Corning confiscated Stanley's portable gaming device. He threw a tantrum and declared in front of everyone that she'd be sorry if she didn't give it back. You think it's some wild coincidence that he happened to spill a bowl of spaghetti on her dress an hour later?"

"Stanley, what do you have to say?"

"Dude, I, like, didn't even know Ms. Corning was sitting there. There was totally milk on the ground. You can ask anyone."

Mr. Sherman stood up and pointed at Stanley. "I bet you spilled the milk yourself before walking back. You see, Principal McKenzie, this boy is undoubtedly guilty."

"No. He's not," said Mikey, causing Mr. Sherman to bare his teeth in frustration. "All you have is circumstantial evidence. Just because someone has a motive to commit a crime, that doesn't mean they're guilty."

"I think you've been watching too many courtroom shows on TV," said Mr. Sherman. "This is the real world."

"But this is *my* school. And in my school, nobody gets punished without indisputable evidence to back it up. Unless you can produce another witness to corroborate your story, Mr. Sherman, we have no choice but to let Stanley go."

Mr. Sherman's face turned so red, it looked like he might transform into a giant tomato. He eyed both boys, then exclaimed, "Fine. If that's the principal's decision, so be it. You may go, Mr. Roberts."

Stanley bolted out of the office before anyone could change their mind.

Mikey turned to Mr. Sherman, saying, "Thank you, I appreciate the—

"Remember one thing, *acting* Principal McKenzie," Mr. Sherman interjected, "I'm the one who's supposed to be principal right now. Not you. Just because some eccentric lady thinks a kid can run the school better than an adult, that doesn't make it true. The minute you lose control, you're going to need me, just like Principal Walker needed me. Then you better hope I feel generous enough to help you."

Mikey could tell Mr. Sherman was trying to win back his dominant position through intimidation. Remembering Principal Walker's advice, he figured the worst thing to do in the situation was to back down and give away the upper hand.

"Mr. Sherman," he retorted, "as you may have heard, school hours are now extended until 3:30 p.m. I need you to phone all the parents and alert them of this within the next half-hour. Thank you."

Mikey leaned back in his chair and put his feet on the desk. Mr. Sherman looked aghast, but muttered, "Of course, sir."

As school ended, Mikey waited out front to be picked up by his mom. Every kid came up to him and shook his hand as they got into their cars as if he were a celebrity. He felt absolutely great.

Stanley Roberts found him and said, "Thanks, Mikey. You saved my butt in there."

"I know," said Mikey. "Especially because you spilled the food on purpose."

"Huh? But you said—"

"How did you know you slipped in milk?" Mikey asked.

"Uhhh, because I … umm …."

"Exactly. I didn't think you would have had time to examine the liquid you slipped in before Mr. Sherman dragged you away. It could have easily been water or soda. You must have left it there yourself, just like Mr. Sherman said."

"But then why did you stick up for me?"

"Because I'm a kid, too. We're still on the same side. Plus, Ms. Corning took away my walky-talky earlier this year and still hasn't given it back, so she had it coming. Next time you might not be so lucky, so keep your nose clean, got it?"

"Got it, Principal. I'll keep my nose clean and my butt clean just for you."

"Stanley, you're a weird kid. But, I like you."

A moment later, Mikey's mom pulled up and shouted out the window, "Let's go, Mikey! You're late for ballet!"

As if they had super-hearing, every kid within three hundred feet burst out laughing like hyenas. How quickly the mighty fall.

During the car ride, Mikey tried to convince his mom that while he was principal, he wouldn't have time for ballet.

"You're crazy," said Tracy. "Ballet is the bomb!"

Thankfully, Mikey was able to persuade his mom to his side. After dropping Tracy off at ballet, she took him to the optometrist (*that's the eye-doctor in case you've never been to one*) for his monthly eye test. Much to his delight, the doctor removed another lens. Now he was down to twenty-one layers. At this rate, he estimated he would be glasses-free before his twelfth birthday.

When he got home, Mikey immediately ran to his computer and connected to Justin via Skype. "Justin, when you finish your homework, I need you to come over."

"What homework?" said Justin. "You abolished it."

"Oh, yeah. Sweet! Come over now so we can brainstorm more ideas."

"I'm way ahead of you, Mikey. I've already worked out

solutions for several of the problems we marked down."

Justin had dinner with Mikey and his family. Afterward they worked out a grand plan for the next day. They spent most of the night on the phone and on websites making all the preparations. Starting tomorrow, life at school would never be the same.

13

Wednesday

The two friends arrived at school as soon as the sun was up and put everything into place. It was sure to be a day no one would ever forget.

Stanley Roberts was the first kid to arrive at school, and as soon as he stepped out of his car, all he could say was "whoa."

Walking around on the school's front lawn were dozens of farm animals!

There were sheep, cows, goats, and pigs, even llamas, ostriches, ponies and deer!

"How do you like it?" said Mikey to Stanley. "The petting zoo across town loaned us their animals for the week."

"Oh man …" said Stanley, trembling with excitement. "I'm freaking out."

"Go pet them," encouraged Justin. "They're all friendly."

"Yeah, uh, okay." Without a second thought, Stanley dropped his backpack and ran as fast as he could to the llamas. He grabbed some feed out of a container and it ate out of his hand.

"Gross! I can feel its tongue!"

After Stanley, all the other kids began to arrive and their joyful reactions were similar to Stanley's. However, when Vice Principal Sherman showed up, it was a different story. Boiling mad, he marched over to Mikey and Justin.

"What in the world is going on here?"

"This is the next step in our plan to improve the students' lives," Mikey explained. "It has been scientifically proven that animals help relieve stress."

"Plus," Justin added, "since the animals need to be fed and cleaned up after, it will teach the students about responsibility and biology." Justin whispered into Mikey's ear immediately after, "Always add in something about learning. Adults love that stuff."

"Hmmph," Mr. Sherman growled. He turned and marched to the front entrance of the school. As he walked through the petting zoo, he stepped in in a pile of goat droppings and howled, "Aghghgh!"

The animals howled back at him.

As Mr. Sherman approached the front entrance, Justin turned to Mikey, "Should we tell him?"

"Nah, let's let him find out on his own."

Mr. Sherman swung open the front doors of the school and upon taking the first step inside, slipped in dramatic fashion, landing right on his bottom. The kids noticed and fell over laughing. Mikey and Justin rushed over to Mr. Sherman and helped him up.

Mikey said, "Sorry, Mr. Sherman, we forgot to tell you. We installed a Slip 'N Slide this morning that runs down the middle of all the school hallways."

Mr. Sherman tried to stand up, but the grease-covered mat beneath his feet was so slippery, he fell down again on his backside.

Mikey continued, "Now kids will never be late for class again because sliding down the hallways is ten times faster than walking."

"But if kids want to walk, they can still use the side walkways," Justin added.

Mr. Sherman rolled off the mat and was finally able to stand up. Greasy slime dripped off his suit. He shot a furious glance at them.

"Don't worry," said Mikey. "The grease is non-staining. I think."

Mr. Sherman swallowed his anger and muttered, "Are there any other booby traps I should know about?"

"No. That should be it," answered Mikey.

"Good."

Mr. Sherman stormed down the hallway, carefully avoiding all the slippery parts. When he turned the corner he let out a bloodcurdling yelp, "Ouuuch!"

"Oh, yeah," Mikey yelled back. "Watch out for those limbo bars. That hallway is an obstacle course now. Forgot we did that!"

Mikey and Justin laughed and high-fived. When the kids came in from the petting zoo, they had the most fun they'd ever had traveling between classrooms. They slid down the hallways like bowling balls rolling down an alley. When they got to the hallway obstacle course, they ducked beneath limbo bars, leapt over hurdles, climbed over a wood barrier, and swung across hanging ropes like Tarzan.

Every kid at Prairie View School was in a fantastic mood when they took their seats in homeroom. No longer were they groggy the rest of the day. They were excited beyond all expectation for what new surprises lay ahead.

Principal Mikey would not disappoint them.

14

For the rest of the morning, Mikey and Justin readied the school for recess. Mikey didn't feel so bad about pulling Justin out of class because he figured they'd be able to catch up using the Class Cam and that would give them another fun activity to do together.

Minutes before the recess bell, sweaty and tired, Mikey and Justin plopped down on a bench by the playground and admired their work.

"Well done, Señor Consultant."

"I can't wait to see the looks on their faces," said Justin.

Mikey reached down into his backpack and handed Mikey an envelope. "Here," said Mikey. "I made this for you."

Mikey handed Justin a badge he had made from the school's art supplies. It was a gold star with the emblem S.C., for Señor Consultant.

The star was cut rather unevenly and the emblem looked kind of cheesy, but Justin was touched nonetheless.

"I'm sorry I made fun of you yesterday," said Mikey. "I couldn't have done this without you."

Pinning the badge on his shirt, Justin replied, "Thanks, Mikey. You have no artistic talent, but I appreciate the effort."

When the recess bell rang, Mikey and Justin led the students out into the play yard. The students' jaws nearly hit the ground when they saw what was there.

Around the entire perimeter, Mikey and Justin had laid down two rows of hundreds of old tires, about ten feet across, creating an amazing course filled with twists and turns.

"Are we going to have a footrace through the course?" one of the seventh-grade boys asked.

"Something like that," said Mikey.

Mikey and Justin proceeded to pull back a tarp, revealing six shiny go-karts! There was a yellow one, a blue one, a red one, a green one, a purple one and an orange one.

Justin stepped forward and announced, "Welcome to the grand opening of the Prairie View Raceway! My uncle was kind enough to donate all of these go-karts and tires. He used to own the Golf N' Fun, but since it closed down, all the go-karts were just sitting in his garage. For those who want to take a spin, form a line and Ms. Tufts will hand you a helmet. You get to make three laps around the track before it's the next person's turn. Enjoy!"

Every student cheered and formed a line in the blink of an eye. Many of the younger students weren't fast enough and ended up way in the back. They were disappointed that they wouldn't get to try the go-karts until lunch, but Mikey and Justin had a plan for them.

Mikey hollered, "Anyone who wants to save the go-karts

for later, follow us!"

A big group of students followed Mikey and Justin to the side of the school. They stood before the outer wall of the school building that stretched two hundred feet. It looked like it hadn't been repainted since the school was built. Splotches the size of dishes had chipped off over the years, exposing the concrete bones of the building. The paint that remained was dirty and faded. It was a perfect symbol of the worn down malaise that had gripped the school before Principal Mikey came along.

Sitting at the base of the wall were twenty buckets of paint in every color imaginable, with trays of brushes in all shapes and sizes.

"This is our school," said Mikey, "so we should be able to make it look how we want. Everyone is free to pick up a brush and paint whatever you like. For anyone who needs help, the art teachers Ms. Bonds and Mr. Beany are here to help you."

The students dashed toward the paint and began creating vivid designs all over the blank wall. It made the students feel good that a part of them would now be part of the school for all to see.

However, that's when Mr. Sherman came sprinting around the corner. "Put down your brushes at once!" he shouted. "This is state property," he huffed at Mikey. "You have no right to paint it without approval!"

"Look at this wall," said Mikey. "Could what the students do possibly make it look any worse? If the state doesn't like it, they can paint it back how it was. But since they wouldn't paint it before, I don't see why they would start now."

Mikey thought Mr. Sherman would blow a gasket, but when he actually took a moment to take in what the students were painting, he seemed to settle down. A third-grader, Chloe Parker, had drawn a bright shining sun above a field of colorful flowers. A fourth-grader, Max Nichols, had painted a baseball field with all his favorite players at each position.

Mr. Sherman seemed to melt at how bright and cheery the students' artwork was. Even *he* didn't have the heart to make them stop. "All right," he said. "I guess they can keep painting. Good work, everyone." But just as he said that, three go-karts zipped past him on the go-kart track. "Ya-hoo!" the racers screamed as they blazed past in the heat of a very close race.

His foul demeanor immediately returned. "Are those go-karts?" he exclaimed in disbelief.

"That's right," said Mikey. "Want to take a ride?"

"No! I think my time would be better spent making the sure the school isn't shut down before lunch. This has gone too far! You hear me? Aghgh!"

Mr. Sherman tugged at his short brown hair as he ran back into the school. Once again, he forgot about the Slip 'N Slide and crashed on his backside, getting a fresh coat of grease on his suit.

"What is the world coming to?" Mr. Sherman shrieked so loud the whole yard heard him.

Justin turned to Mikey and whispered, "Dude, I think Mr. Sherman is losing it."

15

So far, Operation Kids-in-Charge had been an unqualified triumph.

After recess, Mikey kicked back in his big comfy principal's chair and thought about all the happy faces he had seen that day. Whether they were petting a cow, sliding down a hallway, racing a go-kart, or painting a mural, every kid had had a day at school they would never forget.

Mikey could have basked in the glow forever, but in less than a minute, he was fast asleep. Between planning for the day's events and arriving at school at the break of dawn to make the preparations, he had barely slept a wink and it had finally caught up with him.

The lunch bell woke him up.

Mikey ran as fast as he could to the lunch hall. All the students were lined up at the counter where, just as he had promised, the cafeteria cooks cut fresh slices of hot pizza for the hungry students.

Mikey found Justin supervising behind the counter. He made sure that each pizza was a "healthy pizza" topped with vegetables and made with multi-grain dough. "Hey Mikey," said Justin, "I brought the chefs a list of healthy pizza recipes that are even healthier than the usual lunch foods."

"Good job, Señor Consultant," praised Mikey.

Then, from across the room, Mikey noticed a raucous breaking out at one of the tables. The fifth-graders threw food at the sixth-graders, trying to start a food fight. Mikey rushed over.

"What's going on here?" Mikey asked them, sternly.

"It wasn't our fault," said one of the sixth-grade boys. "Those fifth-graders started chucking peas at us first."

"I see," replied Mikey. "You think you can have a food fight under my watch as principal? Well I say ... of course you can! FOOD FIGHT!"

Mikey picked up a big wad of spaghetti and threw it across the table into the faces of two fifth-graders. The fifth-graders responded by heaving all of their spaghetti at Mikey so that noodles covered him from head to foot.

"All right!" proclaimed Mikey. "I'm a spaghetti monster!"

In a matter of moments, perhaps the biggest food fight in the history of the world was on. Peas shot through straws like BBs. Garlic rolls hurled across the room like grenades. Pizzas flew like Frisbees.

The teachers bolted through the doors, seeking cover. Whenever one of them tried to put a stop to the battle, Mikey quickly stopped them and urged everyone to keep going. Not even Mr. Sherman dared to stop it.

The students were having so much fun, they forgot all about the go-karts and spent all of lunch teaming up with friends to perform revolting nutritional assaults and diabolical dietary campaigns. It was glory and glop, triumph and toppings, fervor and filth.

By the end, the worn-out kids were sprawled on the floor, breathing deeply and giggling. All around them, the gastronomic warzone looked like there was an explosion at the world's biggest buffet. Every inch of floor, wall, and ceiling was covered with sauces, cheeses, noodles, and vegetables.

It was absolutely beautiful.

When it was finally safe to return, the teachers reentered the lunch hall and told the kids it was time to get back to class.

Doug Wylie, a popular eighth-grade boy stood up and proclaimed, "The heck with class! Let's ride the go-karts. What can they do? Send us to the principal? He just wants us to have fun!"

The hordes of students cheered Doug's speech and rushed out of the lunch hall to ride the go-karts. The teachers tried to chase them down, but the kids just ran around the yard like it was a game and refused to go to class. Even Justin was out in the yard having fun.

Mikey realized this was not good. The school still needed to function as it was supposed to or else Principal Walker could easily change her mind and replace him with Mr. Sherman.

As if on cue, Mr. Sherman tapped Mikey on the shoulder. "Looks like you've created a monster, Dr. Frankenstein."

Mr. Sherman's analogy couldn't have been more accurate. Mikey had intended to create a school that would be fun *and* a good place learn, but somehow, he had seemed to lose track of that second part.

His creation was out of control.

Not only were the kids go-karting during class time, they had taken the paint supplies and were painting all over the inside of the school. When teachers noticed them scratching their bodies and heads, they checked their scalps and realized that the petting zoo animals had given all of the kids lice! The nurse reported to Mikey that the Slip 'N Slide had so far caused five twisted ankles and six head lumps.

Instead of solving problems like he had promised, all he had done was turn the school into a poorly run, not to mention dangerous, amusement park.

There had to be some way to make the school a bastion of learning, but also an exciting, fun place to be.

Mikey found Mr. Sherman and said the words he thought he would never have to say. "I need your help."

"I've already done what I need to do," replied Mr. Sherman. "A few minutes ago, I left a message for the county superintendent. I didn't want to cause a panic and tell him a ten-year-old kid is running the school, but I did say he needs to visit as soon as possible and see what's going on here."

"That's not fair!" Mikey argued. "It's only my second day on the job! You have to give me more time. I can fix this."

"You better. Or I don't think you're going to last past tomorrow."

16

The day had gone from fabulous to disastrous in what seemed like the blink of an eye. After lunch, none of the kids went back to class and kept on riding the go-karts, petting the animals, and painting the school. Since it was all his idea, Mikey couldn't bring himself to dole out any discipline, and the kids relished their freedom.

Mikey spent the rest of the afternoon trying to figure out how to get things back in order. Luckily, the superintendent hadn't visited the school by the end of the day, so he still had his job.

Justin came over to Mikey's house after school, and they brainstormed ways to restore order without taking away all the fun and excitement. They worked all evening but weren't happy with any of their ideas. Eventually they decided that things would just have to go back to normal as much as possible. Mikey had never felt so defeated.

After Justin left, there was a knock at Mikey's door.

"Hey, Mikey, it's Tracy. Can I come in?"

Surprised, Mikey said, "Sure, sis." She hadn't visited his room in months.

Tracy sat down in his desk chair while Mikey sat on his bed. Tracy looked around at the familiar space-themed posters on Mikey's wall and the dinosaur figurines on his shelf. She seemed bemused as if thinking that Mikey could still be such a little kid in some ways and so adult in others.

"What did you and Justin decide to do?" she asked.

"Everything's going back to normal," Mikey replied. "We couldn't think of anything better."

"That stinks," said Tracy. "Today was probably the most

fun day of school I've ever had."

"Yeah, but Mr. Sherman called the Superintendent and told on us. If the superintendent comes tomorrow and things are the same, both me and Principal Walker will get fired and Mr. Sherman would become the principal."

"No! Mr. Sherman cannot become principal. He'd probably expel me again first thing!"

"I know. That's why I have to put things back to normal. Not only for my sake. For you, too."

Tracy was touched. She could see how much Mikey wanted to protect her and make her happy. She quickly ran to her room and came back with her hamster, Princess.

"Here," said Tracy. "You can play with Princess for the night. She's good at making me feel better."

Mikey was astonished. Tracy never let him play with Princess without her there. Princess crawled onto Mikey's lap and he pet her light brown and white fur. She squeaked and nibbled on his shirt buttons.

"You're right," said Mikey. "She does make me feel better."

As Tracy left the room, she turned around and said, "If it's any consolation, after what you pulled off today, I heard the older kids talking about you in the parking lot, and you definitely earned some cool points."

"Thanks," said Mikey. Tracy smiled and left the room.

Then, a thought flashed into Mikey's head. "That's it!" he said out loud. "Cool Points!"

Thursday

Once again, Mikey and Justin arrived at school before the sun was up. First thing they did was send back all the animals (it was now itchingly clear why the petting zoo was so eager to loan them out) and with great dismay, they dismantled the go-kart track and had the go-karts shipped back to storage. They finished by scrubbing all the paint off the inside of the school and rolling up the Slip 'N Slide. They would have left in the obstacle course, but unfortunately, one of the teachers had pointed out that it was a fire hazard. Ironic considering it was used by firemen as training equipment.

Exhausted by 7:30 a.m., it felt like he had worked a full day before school even began.

When the students arrived at school, they were sad to see that the petting zoo and all the other fun stuff was gone. Mikey directed the downtrodden students to the gym for a special assembly, where he hoped his new ideas would cheer them up.

Before the assembly, Mikey put on his one and only suit and tie. He realized that if the kids were to take him seriously as principal, he had to look the part. He hadn't worn it since last year at his grandparents' 50th anniversary party. He was happy that it was too small for him now. He liked that kind of hard evidence that he was growing.

Mikey stood before the assembled students and faculty. The students hoped to hear about a new kid-friendly policy. As usual, the teachers dreaded the same thing.

"Good morning, everyone. As you have noticed by now, there is no more petting zoo or go-karts. I thought you would be able to handle those privileges and still respect your teachers and schoolwork, but that proved not to be the case. I want you to know that nobody will be getting punished because I blame only myself for what happened. That's why I have come up with a new system. It may not be as fun as animals and racing, but it should make your days far more enjoyable. By a show of hands, who here likes waking up and going to school in the morning?"

Nobody raised a hand.

"Well, that's about to change. While I can't make school start later, since most of your parents need to drop you off before they go to work, what I can do is make the mornings better. Justin, please pass the hats."

Justin handed a baseball cap to a kid on the end of each row.

"In these caps you will find slips of paper. Everyone remove a slip of paper then pass the hat to the person next to you until everyone has taken one."

The students did as Mikey instructed. After they took their slip of paper, they saw that there was writing on it. They read it and looked quizzically at each other.

Mikey pointed to a young girl sitting in the front row. "Becky Armstrong, what does your paper say?"

The third-grader hollered, "It says 'feed the fish.'"

Then Mikey pointed to Jeremy Ramer. "What does yours say, Jeremy?"

"Mine says 'Water the roses.'"

"And yours, Stanley?"

"Clean the iguana cage. Whoa."

"Excellent! What about yours, Tracy?"

Tracy replied, "Make the dough. What does this mean, Mikey?"

"Allow me to explain. Back when I was in first grade, I decided that I didn't want to go to school anymore. I threw a tantrum every morning. Then, my teacher decided to give me a simple job to do in the morning. It was my responsibility to feed the classroom goldfish, Penelope. From that point on, I couldn't wait to get to school because I knew Penelope depended on me for her breakfast. It was like I had my own pet at school. So, from now on, instead of going straight to your homeroom every morning, the first fifteen minutes you'll get to do your special jobs."

Tracy raised her hand. "What does 'make the dough' mean, Principal Mikey?"

The school laughed at Mikey's own sister calling him Principal Mikey.

"You got lucky, sis. Since we're having pizza every day, you get to help the cafeteria chefs make the pizza dough!"

"Oh, cool!"

Mikey turned on a projector hooked up to Justin's laptop. It displayed a new daily schedule on the big screen.

"As you can see, from now on, 8:00 a.m. to 8:15 a.m. is *Special Job Time*."

"And then we have to go to class, right?" Justin yelled out, playing along with the script.

"Wrong!" Mikey clicked, and the next screen to pop up read:

8:15 a.m. to 8:30 a.m. – FIRST RECESS.

The school cheered.

"That's right," said Mikey. "I think all of us feel so groggy in the morning, all we want to do is go back to sleep. We never really feel awake until after we've had our playtime. So I figured, why not move up first recess?"

Even the teachers nodded, as if they thought his ideas weren't so bad after all.

"During first recess," Mikey continued, "you can play in the schoolyard, or if you want, you can finish up your homework. Assuming, of course, that Principal Walker makes us do homework once she returns. If you're ever freaking out because you forget to do your homework, you have a second chance to get it done and your morning can be stress-free."

A skinny seventh-grader named Jeff Prewitt raised his hand.

"Yes, Jeff?"

Mikey prided himself on knowing the names of every student. Last night he'd gone through his old yearbooks and put a name to every face.

"Principal, I'm with you on this first recess thing, but my job says I'm supposed to wash my classroom's windows. What if I don't want to do it?"

"Good question, Jeff. While I always thought it was fun to wash windows because you get to use a squeegee, I understand if others don't share my enthusiasm. But that brings me to my final point of the day."

The screen changed. In big letters it read: *COOL POINTS*

"For our whole lives, adults have controlled us by imposing punishments when we do something bad. If we misbehave, we get a detention. If we get a bad grade, we get grounded. But how often are we rewarded for doing something good? I bet the answer is *rarely*, if ever. Well, with the Cool Points system, I promise that no good deed will ever go unrewarded. By doing your assigned tasks, you will earn yourself a Cool Point as well as a Cool Point for your class. When you get an A on a test, you earn yourself five Cool Points *and* your class five Cool Points."

Mikey flipped to another screen with a chart.

500 Cool Points = 10 points of extra credit.

5,000 Class Cool Points = Class Party Day

"The Cool Points you earn can be put toward any grade you're not happy with. Say for instance you got a seventy on a test. If you earn five hundred Cool Points, you can turn that seventy into an eighty. Plus, when your whole class achieves five thousand points, you all get a party day. You'll get to have ice cream and cake and watch movies during class time."

Jeff replied, "Dude, you had me at squeegee. But I'm liking these Cool Points!"

The students cheered, echoing his sentiments.

"In addition," Mikey continued, "the student who has the most Cool Points at the end of each month wins a gift certificate for your favorite toy store."

That was the topping on the cake. The kids imagined all the cool stuff they could earn just by doing simple tasks and performing well on their schoolwork.

Mikey concluded with, "That's everything I've got for today, but I promise to make more great changes tomorrow. Following this assembly, I've designated fifteen minutes for you to do your first special jobs to start earning some points. I've handed out Cool Points notebooks to all your teachers. They will be keeping track and reporting your progress to me every day. Have a great morning!"

The school gave Mikey another standing ovation. Once again, he began to feel that impulse from deep within. It was telling him to announce that from now on, every day would be *Bring Your Pet to School Day.* He was about do it, but then saw Justin waving a finger at him, implying, *don't you dare.* Mikey thought better of it and made a quick exit out of the gym.

Mikey watched with great satisfaction as the students worked on their special jobs. When they reported back to their teachers, they earned their first Cool Points and felt great by accomplishing a task and receiving a reward.

"I think I'm going to ask to do some of my friends' jobs too," said Marcia Wallace. "I really need to turn that D+ in Math into a C+ before report cards come out."

As the students arrived at their first classes, Mikey settled into his office. He got lost in a daydream about being awarded Man of Year for being the first principal ever to successfully combine fun and learning. That's when the phone on the desk rang, snapping him out of it. Mikey made a quick wish that it wasn't who he thought it might be, but his wish was not answered.

Mikey picked up the phone. "Hello?"

"Hello, this is Superintendent Matthews. To whom am I speaking?"

17

"Hello, Superintendent," said Mikey, not doing a very good job trying to deepen his voice through the phone. "This is Mikey, I mean, Michael McKenzie."

"Hello, Michael. I received a call yesterday that there is a problem at the school. Has it been taken care of or do I still need to make the trip over there?"

"Oh, it's definitely been taken care of. No need to make the trip."

"That's good to hear. Could you please put on Principal Walker? I have something very important to tell her."

"Principal Walker is on leave. I'm the temporary principal."

"I see. I don't believe I know you. What is your position there?"

"I'm the umm ... computer teacher."

"I see. To be perfectly frank, you sound like a ten-year-old kid."

"I know. I get that a lot."

"What happened to Carl Sherman? I thought he was the vice principal."

"He is. But Principal Walker left me in charge."

"Okay then, I'll need you to pass along a very important message to Tabitha for me."

"Sure thing. Who's Tabitha?"

"Tabitha Walker. The principal."

"Of course! I was just joking. I knew that."

"Riiiight. Are you *sure* you're not a kid?"

"Umm ... last I checked. Heh heh."

"Well, Mr. McKenzie, please let Tabitha know that I'm looking over the GAT results of Prairie View School from the end of last year. You seem to have fallen far behind in both reading and math compared to other schools in the state. Unless the school raises its scores next month, we will have no choice but to close down the school and send the kids to other schools where they have a better chance of success."

"What? You're going to close down the school just because our students aren't doing as well as other schools? Wouldn't a better solution be to hire more teachers and decrease class size? How about improving the science and computer facilities. They're such a joke here. We only have one working water fountain!"

"Hey, don't blame me. Blame the geniuses in the capitol."

"And what if the students do really well on next month's GATs?"

"That's the good news. Everything will stay exactly the same. Of course, if they do *superb*, you might be granted a funding increase and get all those things you're asking for, but that's highly unlikely considering the scores I'm looking at. Have a nice day, Mr. McKenzie."

Mikey couldn't believe it. The School Board was applying the same misguided policies as the school. Prairie View would be punished for doing poorly, while success would lead to non-punishment. Perfection was the only means to reward.

No wonder things weren't getting any better.

Mikey dreaded taking the GAT (General Assessment Test). To chart each student's progress, it was administered twice a year—at the beginning of the school year and at the end. They didn't count toward anyone's grades, so not many students tried hard to do well on it.

However, if the kids knew that scoring poorly on the test could lead to the school closing down and being separated from all their friends, they would certainly put in more of an effort. And if doing well meant receiving cool stuff like a new gym or new computers, they might try *really* hard on it.

Mikey wasn't exaggerating when he said the science and computer labs were a joke at the school! In the science lab, there were never enough microscopes to go around. Kids always had to share in groups of four of more. Performing experiments took *forever*.

Want to know how old the school's computers were? Let's put it this way. None of them had USB ports. Most had no means whatsoever of connecting to the internet.

It was bad.

Before second recess, Mikey visited each classroom. The teachers had put up Cool Points charts on the walls. The kids racked up Cool Points by answering questions correctly and behaving properly.

Mikey's favorite moment was when he saw Johnny Gorman shoot a spitball at Lucinda Perry. The teacher took ten Cool Points away from Johnny and five points away from the entire class. Instead of laughing at Johnny's antics, the whole class was mad at him for taking away their Cool Points. Johnny didn't act up again the rest of class.

Mikey's theory was proven correct. The best means of discipline was for the kids to discipline each other through disapproval of bad behavior.

At 10:30 a.m. it was time for second recess. The kids loved having two recess periods before lunch.

Several teachers confessed to Mikey that they were skeptical about the new schedule at first. They didn't think there would be enough time to fit in their lessons with the Special Jobs and First Recess time cutting into the morning. But, they found that the Cool Points system worked so well, they spent far less time disciplining and more time teaching. They had finished their lessons with time to spare!

Mikey told them to stick with it and to let him know if any problems arose. He hadn't seen Justin yet, but eventually found him visiting the cooks in the cafeteria kitchen. They were flipping pizza dough in the air, getting all the fresh pizzas ready for lunch.

Mikey and Justin had a quick meeting, during which Mikey updated Justin on his phone call with the superintendent.

"Wow," said Justin. "You got incredibly lucky that he believed you're an adult with a kid's voice."

"I know. You do a much better old man voice than me. But it sounds like we could have a big problem if the school doesn't pass next month's GATs with flying colors. If the school closes, all the teachers will lose their jobs. I wouldn't mind never seeing Mr. Sherman again, but Mrs. Hughes doesn't deserve this."

"True, but I'm more worried about being sent to a new school. Let me check something." Justin opened his laptop and pulled up a map of the county.

"Oh no," he murmured. "According to these district lines, half the kids at school would get sent to Park View and the other half to Canyon View."

"What's so bad about that?" asked Mikey.

"The problem is that our houses are in different districts. We would have to go to different schools."

"No," said Mikey, feeling a great weight fall upon his shoulders. "We can't let them do that. We have to make sure the school aces the GATs."

"With just a month to prepare and their other school-work to worry about? I wouldn't get your hopes up."

"Stop being such a stick in the mud. I'm making this our most important operation."

Soon after, *Operation Test Busters* was launched. Mikey ran back to the office to begin preparations, but standing in the room was a man he'd never seen before.

He was short and stocky with a bald head and glasses. He wore a dark gray suit and a blue-and-yellow striped tie. He looked like the kind of man who never laughed.

Noticing a nametag pinned to his jacket, Mikey knew exactly who it was.

"Hello," said the man. "Acting Principal Michael McKenzie, I presume?"

Mr. Sherman was standing at the doorway with a superior grin.

Mikey gulped. "Yes, Superintendent Matthews. I am Principal McKenzie.'"

18

The worst-case-scenario had come to pass. Mr. Sherman had clearly ratted him out and now Mikey was face-to-face with the one person who had authority over Principal Walker.

Superintendent Matthews continued, "It is a pleasure to meet you, Mr. McKenzie. Mr. Sherman has just informed me that Principal Walker made you the acting principal while she's gone. Is that true?"

Mikey looked down. He thought about trying to convince the superintendent that he was a little person, but thought the better of it.

"Yes, Superintendent. "

"Well ... this is extremely horrifying. Principal Walker was clearly not in her right mind when she made the decision."

"That's not true! I gave her ideas on how to improve the school. She knew I would be the only one with enough guts to enact them."

"Having good ideas does not qualify one to be in charge of the welfare of both students and teachers. Right now, everyone is in a very dangerous situation."

"Dangerous? I stopped the school's flu epidemic. I may have saved everyone's lives!"

"Mr. Sherman informed me you installed a go-kart track and several students were injured."

"Not from the go-karts. It was the Slip 'N Slide."

"The slip and what?"

"Look," said Mikey, "that was just a one-day experiment, everything is back to normal now. Actually, if you look around, you'll see it's even better than normal."

"Yes, I'm sure it is," said the superintendent, rolling his eyes. It was the classic gesture Mikey came to expect from an adult not taking him seriously. "I only hope there's enough time to undo the damage that's already been done."

Mr. Sherman butted in, "The first thing he did was abolish homework."

"You abolished homework? This is exactly what I was afraid of."

"That's not exactly true, Superintendent. I just made it optional. Trust me, the kids will start doing homework in order to earn Cool Points."

"Cool *what*?"

As if on cue, Justin burst into the room shouting, "Mikey! Mikey! I formed a hypothesis for Operation Test—hey who's this guy?"

"This is Superintendent Matthews."

"Oh. Good day, Superintendent. If you don't mind, Principal Mikey and I have important work to do."

"Who is this kid?" asked the superintendent, incredulously. "The school nurse?"

"This is Señor Consultant Justin Gluck, my right-hand man," Mikey answered.

"Oh, this just keeps getting better. The second in command is another kid? I'm surprised they haven't turned the library into an arcade!"

"What's an arcade?" Mikey and Justin said together.

"You know, a big room with a bunch of video games."

"Ohhh, right," said Justin. "I've heard of those. They were popular before they invented home gaming systems."

"Weird," said Mikey. "But now that he mentions it, maybe it's not such a bad idea. We should have a video game room in the school where students can use their Cool Points to earn playing time."

"That's a great idea!" Justin responded.

"NO! IT'S A TERRIBLE IDEA!" Superintendent Matthews shrieked, shaking in his penny loafers. "School is no place for video games!"

"How about we compromise," said Mikey, brushing off the superintendent's tantrum. "Let's just have a room where they can play educational games during recess?"

"No!" shouted the superintendent.

"Hey, that's actually not such a bad idea," Mr. Sherman chimed in, surprisingly.

"I said, no! I'm the boss here! I will not stand for this silliness one more minute!"

"Justin," said Mikey under his breath, "Mr. Matthews says that he's going to have to fire me. Could you please check on that?" Mikey finished with a wink so that Justin understood the message.

"Gotcha. I'll be right back."

Justin bolted out of the room, leaving Mikey alone with the two adults.

"Now," said Superintendent Matthews, "let's not waste any more time and formally make Vice Principal Sherman the acting principal. I'll just need you to sign this form, transferring your power to Mr. Sherman. If you sign it right now, *maybe* you won't be in big trouble."

Mikey needed to buy a few more minutes, but didn't want to give Superintendent Matthews any due cause for firing him. So he pretended to go along with it.

"All right," said Mikey. "It was fun while it lasted. Give me the form so I can read it over. Then I'll sign it."

Mikey examined the writing on the one-page form for a full minute. Then another minute. And another.

"What's taking so long?" prodded the superintendent, impatiently. "Just sign the form!"

"Hey! I'm only ten years old. I'm a slow reader. Give me time to finish."

"Ugh! No wonder the test scores are so low at this school."

In reality, Mikey had finished reading the form in the first thirty seconds, but he just needed to buy enough time for …

"Don't you dare sign that form!" Justin commanded, bursting into the room. "According to state and county law, the superintendent is not allowed to remove you from duty without due cause and the majority consent of the School Board."

Justin had used the time to search the procedures for superintendents removing principals from power. As Mikey expected, Justin had become an expert on the subject in mere minutes.

"But I have due cause! He's ten years old!"

"Excuse me? That's age discrimination! My dad is a litigator. If you fire Mikey based solely on those grounds, we will have you and the entire School Board tied up in motions and depositions for the next five years. My dad *never* loses."

Superintendent Matthews was speechless. He looked over at Mr. Sherman, but the vice principal whistled casually and walked out of the room. He didn't want to get dragged into any lawsuit.

"I see," said Superintendent Matthews. "If that's the way you want to play, I was hoping not to involve the School Board in a matter as silly as this. When I alert them about what's been done, not only will they give me permission to fire Mikey, they will order me to fire Principal Walker as well. Good day to the both of you."

Superintendent Matthews straightened his tie, picked up his briefcase, and exited the office.

"Thanks, Justin," said Mikey. "You're a life-saver."

"You got it, but we better get to work. As soon as he meets with the School Board, we could be out of a job."

"You're right. There's no time to waste. We gotta bring in the rest of our good ideas first thing tomorrow, cause we probably won't have another chance."

19

Mikey and Justin agreed to meet after school. They had a lot of work ahead of them. They had to formulate a plan for *Operation Test Busters* as well as brainstorm all their best ideas and policies to be put into place the next day.

The minute school let out at 3:30 p.m., Justin entered Mikey's office. "Hey, I'll meet you at your place at five, okay?"

"At five?" said Mikey. "I already told my mom I was going straight home with you. We have too much to do."

"Yeah, but we have that test tomorrow."

"Test? What test?"

"On Lewis and Clark."

"*Lois* Lane and *Clark* Kent?"

"Dude, you're in really deep trouble. Haven't you been watching our lessons on the Class Cam?"

"I've been way too busy!"

"Well you better get on it. You're gonna have to know all the founding fathers' names, what states they were from, and—"

There was a knock at the door.

Mikey said, "Come in."

Stanley Roberts entered.

"Hey, dudes. Uhhh … Mikey … did you, like, see what's going on outside?"

Mikey and Justin walked through the school's front entrance into the late afternoon daylight. The entire street was filled with news vans. There must have been dozens of newscasters with camera crews in tow.

One of the newscasters saw Mikey and shouted, "There he is!"

There was a mad dash toward him.

Mikey and Justin rushed back inside while the ravenous newscasters mobbed the front entrance. They pounded on the doors and begged Mikey to come back out.

Catching his breath, Justin huffed, "This is the work of the superintendent. He must have alerted the media so there would be a public outcry to have you removed."

"Maybe. It could have also been Mr. Sherman."

"It doesn't matter. We have to find a way to sneak you out of here. Those news people will eat you alive."

"Wait, you don't think I could handle their questions?"

"Trust me, Mikey. All they want to do is make a fool out of you. Even if you answer every question perfectly, they'll edit it to make you look bad."

"But if I run away, it'll look like I have something to hide. Like I'm a chicken."

"It's better than accidentally saying the wrong thing that could give Superintendent Matthews grounds to fire you. All he needs is the slightest little mistake."

Mikey took a moment and weighed his options. Justin was probably right. But then again, a leader who can't stand up to public scrutiny is no real leader.

If he was the right man for the job, the news had the right to ask questions. It was his job to prove himself.

"You can go home, Justin. I'm going to stay here and answer their questions."

"But, Mikey—"

"That's an order."

Justin shook his head in exasperation.

Mikey added, "Don't worry. I'll be careful. See you at five at your place."

Justin walked out the front entrance. The press ignored him as he walked past. Mikey took a deep breath and opened the doors.

Like a wave crashing down upon him, the newscasters charged with a barrage of questions. There were so many voices and flashing lights, Mikey couldn't understand a single word they were saying.

One of the microphones hit Mikey on the head, knocking his glasses onto the ground. After putting them back on, an invigorated Mikey screamed at the top of his lungs, "BE QUIET!"

The press immediately became silent, waiting to hear what he would say.

"You all behave worse than third-graders. If any student acted like such out-of-control animals in *my* school, they would get sent straight to detention. Now, here's how this is going to work. I want everyone to line up single-file."

The newscasters looked at one another in confusion.

"What are you waiting for? Line up!"

Grumbling, the embarrassed newscasters managed to arrange themselves in an orderly line, extending all the way across Prairie View's front lawn.

"Good job," said Mikey. "Now, each one of you is going to be allowed to come into my office *one by one* for a five-minute interview. All of you will get your chance, so everyone should be happy."

The press nodded their heads and appeared happy with the arrangement. Mikey got the sense that they were actually impressed by his leadership.

For the rest of the afternoon, Mikey engaged in interviews in his office. He explained to them how he had solved the flu epidemic by tracing it back to the germy water fountain. He illuminated them with his reasoning for extending the lunch period and P.E. He illustrated the Cool Points system and how he was already seeing positive results.

During one interview, Mikey said, "Kids are living in a video game culture these days. Schools should take advantage of that by installing a point-earning system that we're used to. We'll relate the fun of video games to the tasks of school. Talk about a whole new outlook!"

He encouraged the interviewers to speak with the teachers to verify how well the system was working.

There were, of course, some rough patches. One of the interviewers asked Mikey if he felt he had made any mistakes. Mikey admitted that he may have acted hastily in abolishing homework as his first act as principal. But he thought he made up for it by making homework an optional task of the Cool Points system. He expected the students to do more homework than they ever had before in order to earn points.

The most uncomfortable moment came when an interviewer had somehow found out about his sister and asked Mikey if he thought it was unfair that he reversed his own sister's expulsion.

Mikey countered by asserting, "The punishment was excessive for a first-time violation. I would have done the same thing for any other student."

All in all, Mikey felt the interviews went very well. The only problem was, when Mikey started talking, he often found it difficult to stop. Though he tried to limit them to five minutes each, the interviews lasted at least fifteen minutes. He was enthralled that adults were finally taking him seriously.

The last interviewer finished by saying, "Thank you for the interview. I must say, this is a very odd town. On the way here our news van got into a fender-bender because I could have sworn I saw a bunch of squirrels walking across a tightrope high above the street."

Mikey laughed, "Yeah, that's … weird." Then, he looked at the clock and was immediately horrified. It was 7:15 p.m. He had completely lost track of the time.

Mikey called his Mom to come pick him up. The press had a field day, laughing as the school principal was picked up by his mommy.

After being dropped off at Justin's, Mikey knocked on the front door. When Justin saw Mikey standing in the doorway, he scowled at him. Then, he slammed the door in his face.

20

Mikey was beyond confused. Sure, he was a few hours late, but Justin must have understood that he had a good excuse.

Mikey banged on the door again, thinking Justin must be playing a joke on him. Justin opened the door. The look on his face was still dead serious.

"Go home, jerk," he said. "You're not welcome here."

"I'm sorry" said Mikey. "It's not my fault I'm late. The interviews lasted longer than I thought they would. You don't have to freak out about it."

"I don't care that you're late, stupid. You know what you did."

"No. I don't."

"Oh, really? Let's just watch the interviews then."

Justin pulled Mikey into the living room. He brought up the DVR menu on the TV screen. Justin had recorded all of Mikey's interviews on the various channels.

Mikey watched each interview and thought he came across quite well. He listened for something that may have insulted Justin, but couldn't spot a thing.

"Well?" Justin prodded. "Now do you get it?"

"No. I don't see what you're so mad about. I never even mentioned your name."

"Exactly! You just sat there and took all the credit for everything as if I didn't even exist. Listen to yourself. '*I* solved the flu epidemic ... *I* extended the lunch period ... *I* created the Cool Points system.' You know darn well at least half, if not more, of those ideas came from me. Well guess what? If you think you can do it all yourself without me, then go ahead. I quit."

Mikey realized that Justin was right. He had felt so high and mighty during the interviews that he had completely forgotten to give Justin even the slightest bit of credit.

"I'm sorry," said Mikey. "I messed up. Maybe I can call the stations and do another interview."

"It's too late. My whole family came over to watch you on the news. I told them you would mention my name for sure. But you never did. You made me look like a fool."

Justin took the Señor Consultant badge out of his pocket that Mikey had made for him. He slammed it in Mikey's hand.

"Take it. If you think you can run the school without my help, go ahead."

Mikey was angry that Justin not only hadn't accepted his apology, but gave back the badge that he had spent almost twenty minutes crafting for him.

"Fine! I can run the school without you. You know, I didn't have to bring you along. I only did because you were my friend. But I guess you don't appreciate it."

Mikey stormed out of the house and ran all the way back home. He held back his tears, not wanting to give Justin the satisfaction.

But as he ran, the addresses and street signs started to get blurry.

Inside his room at home, Mikey heard a knock on the door. He had been crying for thirty minutes and figured his mom must have heard him.

"Come in," he said.

Tracy walked into the room.

"Oh. Hi, Trac'."

Embarrassed, Mikey quickly wiped away the tear tracks on his face.

"It's okay, Mikey. Remember when you came into my room the other day when I was crying? You may not have realized it, but you made me feel better just by caring enough to talk to me. What's wrong?"

"It's Justin," Mikey said. "He's not my friend anymore."

"Really? But aren't you, like, each other's only friend?"

Tracy made a funny face that made Mikey chuckle a little through his sobs.

"You know," Tracy continued, "if it's your new job that's the problem, you could always quit. It's not worth losing a friendship over."

"Maybe you're right," Mikey said. "I don't know."

"I mean, nobody would blame you. You've done so much already. I appreciate what you did for me, but you're just a kid. You're not supposed to have this kind of pressure."

"But I still have so much to do. I can make things even better. I know it."

"Mikey, what I'm saying is. I want you to quit."

"Why?" asked Mikey, taken aback.

"I know things seem great when you're around, but kids are only acting good in front of you because you're the principal. When you're not around, they've been mean to me. They're calling me really bad names. I think things would go back to normal if you went back to being a student."

"Oh, I get it. This was never about me. This is about *you*. I'm trying to do good things, and you can't take being teased for a couple of measly weeks? Well, welcome to *my* life! Get out!"

Tracy gritted her teeth like she wanted to punch Mikey, but just turned and left the room. Mikey felt bad after he realized he had taken out his anger toward Justin on his sister.

He collapsed on his bed, trying as hard as he could to block out his emotions. He needed to think of a great idea for what might be his last day on the job if the super-intendent had his way. It was very difficult to concentrate, though, as Justin's words echoed in his head: *You just sat there and took all the credit!*

Then, Mikey sprang out of bed with another epic idea. "That's it!" he said aloud. "Credit!"

21

Friday

Mikey arrived at school a half hour early at 7:30 a.m. He had emailed every teacher the night before to meet him in the library for an emergency presentation.

Once again, he had to fight his way through a sea of photographers and newscasters. The story had really caught on. There was an even bigger crowd than before. Mikey wished Justin were there to fend them off. He ran as fast as he could through the sea of photographers. Luckily, they weren't allowed to follow him inside the school.

Mikey caught his breath and straightened his suit. His mom had it tailored so it now it fit him perfectly.

It was time to enact what he felt would be his most important policy and lasting legacy. There was no time to lose as Superintendent Matthews could enter at any moment and remove him from his post.

The faculty was gathered in the library. They seemed excited to hear Mikey's new ideas. Mr. Sherman stood in back, keeping a skeptical ear open.

"Ladies and gentlemen," said Mikey, addressing the teachers seated before him. "Let's talk about ... *extra credit*."

The teachers leaned forward in their seats.

"We are going to install a whole new system that involves the students learning independently outside the classroom and beyond the textbooks. But first, let me tell you about a few things I've learned. At the center of our galaxy there's a black hole that's four million times as massive as the sun. It's swallowing up stars and growing more massive by the second. I learned that fact when I was eight years old because I looked up at the night sky and wondered what was out there. So, I picked up a book and read all about it. Last year, we had a test on the state capitals in geography class. I knew them all by heart and got 100% on the test. Somebody ask me what the capital of North Dakota is."

Mrs. Hughes obliged, "What's the capital of North Dakota?"

"I have no idea," Mikey replied. "I've forgotten. In fact, I think I've forgotten all of the state capitals except for Washington, D.C."

"It's not a state capital. It's the nation's capital," Mrs. Hughes corrected.

"Precisely my point. Last night I realized that everything that I've learned on my own has stuck inside my head like permanent glue. But, everything I was forced to memorize to pass a test has left my brain like a cloud evaporating in the sky. Can any of you guess why this is?"

None of the teachers raised their hands. Mikey was getting a kick out of asking the teachers questions as if they were kids in a classroom. He thought about calling on one who clearly didn't know the answer just so they would see what it felt like, but decided against it.

"Okay, I'll tell you why. According to my research, it all has to do with how the human brain works. When we learn something on our own, the brain stores the information in its long-term memory bank. But, when we are forced to learn about something just for a test, it gets stored in the brain's short-term memory bank, because the brain has decided that the information is not interesting or useful beyond the test date. Therefore, it gets put in a place where it can be quickly forgotten about once the test is over."

The teachers began to understand, but they started to get nervous that a big change was heading their way.

"This brings me to my new policy," Mikey divulged. "From now on, we must encourage as much extracurricular learning as possible. In exchange for any outside learning a student performs they must be rewarded with either extra-credit points or a homework pass. Assuming the kids have to do homework once Principal Walker comes back."

The teachers chuckled. A fourth-grade teacher, Mrs. Clancy, raised her hand. "I'm confused. How do we know the kids are learning outside of school to give them the extra-credit?"

"I'm just getting to that. Each student will be able to get extra-credit by completing projects about the current subjects they are learning. You should let them choose stuff that play to their strengths. For instance, if you are currently teaching the Civil War, the good writers in the class may choose to write an essay, or a poem, or even a song about the Civil War. The performers may choose to perform a skit for the class. The artists may draw a scene from the Gettysburg Address or even a comic strip that illustrates something they've learned. It will be up to you to award the amount of extra-credit each kid deserves."

The teachers seemed to like the idea.

"Now," Mikey continued, "this next part might be a little bit harder to swallow. The students should also be able to earn extra credit on every quiz and every test you give them. A big test, for instance, usually takes a full forty-five minutes of class time. From now on, you must design your tests to take no longer than thirty minutes. The remainder of the time must be allocated for students to write down everything else they have learned about the subject that was *not* on the test. Whether it's simple facts, dates, or an extra essay."

"Wait," Mrs. Hughes piped in, "doesn't that mean if a student already got one-hundred percent on a test, he or she could earn well past a perfect score? Even up to two hundred percent?"

"Yes. And imagine how good that student would feel should they earn such a mark. I also imagine that some students may get only a D on the first part of the test, then be able to raise it to a B or an A with enough extra-credit work. I can understand why you might think that sounds silly, but I implore you to ask yourselves a fundamental question: *Why are you teaching these kids*? Is it purely to grade them and fit them into categories of good test-takers and bad test-takers? Or, do you teach them so that they can gain as much knowledge as possible in a subject? Perhaps even inspire a love for it? I think if a student displays super-crazy knowledge on a subject in the extra-credit section, even though he or she may not have known the answers to the questions you chose to ask, then that student deserves a good grade."

The room was silent. A sixth-grade teacher, Mr. Clark, raised his hand. "I think this is a very interesting idea, Principal Mikey, but what happens if everyone in the entire class gets *over* one-hundred percent by doing all that extra credit?"

"Mr. Clark, if that happens, I hope that it is the proudest day of your teaching career. It would mean that every single student was inspired enough to spend extra time outside of your assignments to learn about the subject and exceed all expectations. It means they will have acquired knowledge on their own that they will hold for a lifetime. If everyone in your class deserves an A, then everyone *should* get an A. If your students perform well, they will consequently enjoy school more, which will lead to a lifetime love of learning and far greater success in high school and college."

The teachers rose out of their seats and applauded. Mikey felt amazing. However, his joy was somewhat diminished not having Justin by his side to share it.

"Now," said Mikey. "I have to—"

"Wait!" Mr. Sherman interrupted from the back of the room. "Principal Mikey, before this meeting adjourns, I have an idea I'd like to share."

Mikey gulped, expecting the worst. "Yes, Mr. Sherman?"

Mr. Sherman held up a video game console. "I decided to donate my old Xbox to the school. You mentioned yesterday that you thought it might be a good idea for the kids to use their Cool Points to play educational video games during recess."

Mikey's jaw dropped. It was one thing for Vice Principal Sherman to support one of his ideas, but he couldn't believe that he actually played video games.

"You ... you have an Xbox?" said Mikey, flabbergasted.

"Of course. I played *Call of Duty* every day when I was in the army. I just upgraded mine at home, but this one still works great."

"Umm … sure, Mr. Sherman. You take charge and set it up. Good work."

Mikey saw Mr. Sherman smile warmly for the first time. "Yes, sir," he replied, giving Mikey a salute.

"All right, once the students finish their morning tasks, please gather them in the gym for my next big announcement."

"Not so fast," said Mrs. Hughes. "You have a test in American History to take."

Mikey froze. He had completely forgotten about the test.

22

Mikey tried to convince Mrs. Hughes to delay his taking the test until the afternoon, but she wouldn't hear of it.

Since he hadn't studied for a single minute, Mikey was what's known as: up the creek without a paddle.

He had no choice but to push his presentation to the students to second recess. Following first recess, Mikey sat down with the rest of the class to take the test, hoping what little knowledge he had on the American Revolution would be enough to get him through it. He quickly realized it would not.

In the past, Mikey would have been terribly upset after turning in a test he knew he had failed, but this time there was a sense of relief knowing that he would be able to do extra credit to earn the points back.

He may have been "up the creek," but at least he had a spare paddle to save his skin.

After finishing the test, Mikey returned to his office. He prepared his notes for the big announcement to the students. For the first time, he felt extremely nervous. He wasn't sure how the students would take his ideas and imagined being hit by a chorus of boos. The new changes would not be so kid-friendly as his last ones, but he felt the students would appreciate them in the long run.

That's when Mikey noticed a blinking light indicating a message on the answering service. Mikey was petrified that it was Superintendent Matthews telling him the School Board had already voted to remove him.

He pushed the button, saying a quick prayer that it was

from anyone other than the superintendent.

Mikey held his breath and listened: *"You have one …
new message … sent … today at … 9:16. a.m."*

"Hi, Mikey. It's Principal Walker."

Mikey exhaled in relief.

*"I'm just calling to let you know how proud I am of you.
I've been in contact with a few teachers. They said you had
a rough start but have been very impressed with how you
turned it around. While your changes have been rather
… unique … they seem to be working, so keep doing what
you're doing. Don't let anything stand in your way. Oops, I
have a doctor calling on the other line. My mother is fighting
really hard, so I need all your thoughts and prayers. I'll check
back in as soon as I can. Toot-a-loo!"*

The principal's message gave him a boost of confidence. He felt ready to address the students, who were already waiting for him in the gym. Then, an instant message
popped up on the screen from Superintendent Matthews.

It said, *On my way over. Don't go anywhere.*

Mikey ran to the gym as fast as he could. There was no
time to lose.

Moments later, Mikey stood at the podium facing the
entire student body. He scanned the crowd and saw Justin
sitting way in back with his arms crossed and an angry look
on his face. He wished Justin were standing next to him, but
he knew he had to press on without him.

"Good morning, students and teachers," Mikey announced. "I'm going to tell you something right now that
others thought you were too fragile to hear. We've all tak-
en the GATs twice a year and we never really cared that
much because they didn't count toward our grades. But as

it turns out, the school board uses the scores to determine a school's fate. How much money it gets, and even whether it stays open. The schools with the best scores get the most money. The schools with the lowest scores receive the least amount of money and can even get shut down."

A young boy's voice yelled out, "Get to the point, Principal Poindexter!"

"Who said that?" Mikey said into the microphone.

Justin stood up. "I did," he declared indignantly.

Mikey replied harshly, "You disrespected the principal, Mr. Gluck. That's a week's detention."

"Oh, shove it! I'm three months older than you! You can't discipline *me*!"

"Mr. Sherman, please remove that disruptive student from the gym so we may continue."

Everyone's jaws dropped as Mr. Sherman pulled Justin out of the gym. They couldn't believe that the inseparable friends had been driven apart overnight. Mikey took a moment to gather his thoughts.

"As I was saying, what nobody told you is that our GAT scores are the lowest in the state."

There was a murmur among the crowd.

Mikey continued, "If we don't show major improvement on next month's test, the school is going to be shut down and most of us will be split up and sent to different schools."

The crowd gasped. Many looked on the verge of tears, as if their fate were already determined.

"But I don't want you to worry," said Mikey, reassuringly. "Worrying is *my* job." There was a laugh that broke the tension. "This is just another problem that needs to be solved, and solving problems is what I do best. Unfortunately, the only viable solution is that we must significantly raise each of our scores in order to save the school. I have a three-point plan on how we can do this. Some of these ideas probably won't be as popular as my other changes, but it's what I believe must be done to save our school."

Mikey projected his plan on the screen behind him.

Point one. Extra work for extra credit.

"From now on, everyone will have the opportunity to earn extra credit on their subjects by doing work outside of the normal assignments. You will be able to use your smarts, talents, and creativity in all sorts of different ways to show what you've been learning on your own. If enough of us do the extracurricular learning on each of our subjects, I think we will zoom ahead of the other schools in no time. Plus, every test will now be two-thirds graded test, and one-third extra-credit."

There were no enthusiastic cheers, but he wasn't really expecting it. It seemed like all that the students heard was that they would have to do more work outside the class-room. Mikey couldn't waste more time explaining it.

"Let's move on. *Point two. No more bullying.*"

This time there was a smattering of unsure applause from the crowd.

"You may be wondering what bullying has to do with our school's test scores. I can tell you from experience as some-one who has probably gotten bullied as much as anyone, that it can and does affect your schoolwork. Last year, I was getting picked on so much for being 'brainy,' that I decided to get nothing but C's and D's for a whole semester, just so it would stop. Bullying, teasing, and name-calling not only hurts feelings, it takes away confidence and dignity. When that happens, it becomes much harder to succeed at any-thing, especially school work. Girls are just as guilty as boys at this. Sure, you may not hit as much, but when you make fun of other people, call them names, or exclude them from activities, it can be just as hurtful."

Mikey found his sister in the crowd and gave her a wink. It was her past experiences that gave him this idea. She used to come home from school crying at least three times a week because girls in her class had been mean to her. Now she was so eager for acceptance, that she had been manip-ulated into doing bad things.

Mikey finished with conviction so they knew he was serious. "Therefore, we are going to enforce much stricter rules when it comes to bullying. If you are caught bullying, the penalty is a one-day suspension. The second time you bully, it's a week suspension. The third time, you're out. Expelled."

There was a gasp from the crowd and definitely a mixture of feelings. The ones who got bullied a lot were thrilled. They didn't want to make a scene, though. It could possibly upset the bullies. The ones who liked to tease and intimidate the other kids realized this was bad news for them.

Only one person clapped. Everyone turned around and saw it was Mr. Sherman, who had reentered with Justin by his side.

Mikey continued, "Here's what it comes down to: Treat others the way you want to be treated. A bully-free campus will allow everyone to be themselves without feeling too scared to overachieve."

It looked like a dark cloud of uncertainty had swept over the crowd. Everyone wondered if a bully-free school was really possible. Mikey wanted to end on a high note.

"Lastly is Point Three. Every day …"

Suddenly the gym doors burst open. Superintendent Matthews entered along with twelve other men and women wearing sashes that said: *School Board*.

23

Mikey paused at the interruption of Superintendent Matthews with the entire school board.

"Sorry to interrupt," Superintendent Matthews said with fake politeness. "Please, continue."

Mikey wasn't sure what was happening. They must have come to fire him. He decided to make his final point as fast as he could before they had a chance to get rid of him.

"Point three," said Mikey. "Every day at lunch, there will be cake for dessert!"

The students finally cheered. He looked over and saw the school board members with their mouths agape. The superintendent smiled, smugly.

"Yes..." Mikey continued. "Every day there will be *carrot* cake for dessert. It's my favorite. The beta-carotene in carrots will improve our eyes, making it easier to read, which shall also raise our test scores. Thank you! Enjoy the rest of the day."

The cheers turned to boos. It appeared not many of the kids liked carrot cake.

Superintendent Matthews waved Mikey over to him. Mikey shuffled toward him slowly. He felt like a prisoner walking to his execution.

"Principal McKenzie, so good to see you again. These are the distinguished members of the School Board. You made quite an impression on TV last night. It seems that your ideas went over very well with parents in the community. Despite my recommendation to have you removed at once, the board has decided to spend the next two days observing your unconventional policies in action. Then, we will make a decision. Is that agreeable?"

"Sure," said Mikey. "Go ahead. I'm Principal Mikey McKenzie. I'll be in my office if you have any questions. Nice to meet you all."

The board members smiled warmly, then quickly became serious as they pulled out clipboards and pencils, ready to mark down anything that went wrong.

For the rest of the day, the School Board observed Prairie View under Mikey's leadership.

They stood in the back of classrooms and witnessed kids fervently participating in discussions to earn Cool Points. They certainly didn't seem like kids with the lowest test scores in the state.

During lunch, a batch of fresh, hot pizzas came out of the oven. The board members expected a mad scramble, but the students lined up in an orderly fashion so they wouldn't lose points for their class.

When the kids hit the playground and played sports after lunch, there wasn't a single fight, because no one wanted to be mean to someone else and risk getting suspended.

One sixth-grader named Jimmy Bower tried to test the no-bullying rule and pushed a fourth-grader to the ground when he dropped a football pass. The yard teacher saw what happened and sent him straight to Mikey, who gave him a one-day suspension on the spot. Nobody else tested the rules after that.

The school board was impressed by Mikey's surprising toughness. Maybe he was actually making school a better place, and not just creating a kid's dreamland, they appeared to be thinking.

Monday

The following Monday, the members of the School Board arrived early to continue their observations. Every kid arrived on time for school and hurried to their appointed tasks to earn their first Cool Points of the day. Some picked up trash, some mopped the floors, some watered the plants, some mowed the lawn, some helped prepare lunch, and some fed the hamsters, the fish, the snakes, the turtles, or the iguana named Iggy.

As a result, the campus looked immaculate. Just a week before, it had looked like an eight-year-old's room that hadn't been cleaned in a month, complete with graffiti and a strange sticky film on the hallway floor.

Now it looked like a museum of learning. The board members even seemed to approve of the mural the kids had painted on the outer wall. They were overheard talking about letting the kids do that at every school!

During recess, a group of seventh-graders used their Cool Points to play Xbox on the system that Mr. Sherman had donated. Mr. Sherman did a great job setting everything up. He brought a bunch of games that were fun and educational. Everyone looked to be having a great time playing with Mr. Sherman on multi-player mode.

Mikey was most shocked when he saw Mr. Sherman with his tie loosened and acting like a kid. Who knew he had it in him?

Students had already begun to take advantage of the extra credit opportunities. The drama kids put on a play about the pilgrims landing on Plymouth Rock. They scored extra points for using new words that they learned in English class.

It inspired the rest of the kids to think of their own extra credit projects to work on over the weekend.

Several board members interviewed Mikey. He found that he was even more confident than he was in the press interviews. Superintendent Matthews tried to catch Mikey off-guard in front of the School Board by questioning his decision to abolish homework. Mikey had done more research and explained that the country with the number one ranking for education in the world was Finland, where schools have very little or no homework because they would rather have them focusing on extra-curricular activities, sports, socializing, or family bonding after school. But, he noted that most of the kids at Prairie View had already been doing homework voluntarily in order to earn Cool Points.

All in all, Mikey thought the School Board's visit couldn't have gone better. There were no major mishaps, no food fights, no fire alarms, no teacher strikes, no hurricanes, and not one student was out sick with the flu.

However, for those very stressful two days, Justin still refused to speak to Mikey or even acknowledge his existence. Mikey wished more than anything that he had his friend there to share in the glory, but it appeared Justin no longer wanted to be friends.

After completing their inspection on Tuesday afternoon, the board informed Mikey that they would discuss their findings and come back with a decision the next day. Mikey would either be allowed to continue as acting principal or be fired and replaced.

Before leaving, Superintendent Matthews stayed behind and said, "Listen, Mikey. I don't want you to get your hopes up. This inspection was really just for show. The truth is, there's no chance the board will let you remain principal. It's just not safe for a kid to be in charge."

"What do you mean, 'not safe'?" replied Mikey, somewhat offended.

"What if there's an emergency?"

"Hey, I've gone through fire drills, earthquake drills, and tornado drills five times a year since I was three. I know the procedures like the back of my hand."

The superintendent clearly didn't feel like arguing with a small boy, so he turned around and left.

Mikey knew he should have felt ecstatic with how well everything went. He may not have convinced the superintendent, but the board truly seemed impressed with how well the school was operating. Yet, deep down, Mikey felt empty.

He had proven that he could run the school fine without Justin, but he realized that he didn't want to. What made the job fun wasn't thinking of all the new rules and implementing them, nor was it having the power to discipline wrong-doers and reward the virtuous.

What made the job fun was that he was sharing an activity with his best friend. Solving problems by himself was gratifying, but solving problems with Justin was better than a year's supply of chocolate donuts.

For the last two days, being principal had felt like a job instead of a fun project. He wasn't sure he would be able to make it through the next week if his heart was no longer in it.

Once again, he was facing a problem he had no idea how to solve. His only real friendship had ended, and the irony was that Justin was the only one who could help him solve it.

He was about to leave for home when there was a knock at the office door. "Come in," Mikey said excitedly, hoping it would be Justin. But when he saw the frail gloved hand turn the handle, he knew it wasn't him.

"Hello, Mikey," said Mrs. Hughes.

"Hi, Mrs. Hughes," said Mikey. "I was just leaving. Did you need something?"

"Well," said Mrs. Hughes in her soft, wispy voice, "I have the score from your history test if you're interested."

Mikey exhaled deeply. The last thing he wanted was more bad news going into the weekend.

"How did I do?" Mikey asked.

"Oh, you did awful," she said. "Worst score in the class, by far. An F would be generous. I imagine you'll be doing a great deal of extra-credit work this weekend to make up for it. But I thought you might like to know that the second worst grade in the class was a B+. That's the first time I've ever had a class do so well on a history test before. I think it's no doubt due to all your new changes."

"Thanks for letting me know. It makes me feel a little better."

"You look sad, Mikey. Can I ask what's wrong?"

"Nothing. It's just ... um ... principal stuff."

"Really? It has nothing to do with Justin?"

"How did you know?"

"I may be getting old, but I'm not blind. You two haven't spoken in days. And both of you have the same dreary looks on your faces. Would you like to talk about it?"

Mikey did want to talk about it. He had been holding it in for so long he was ready to burst. He found that he liked talking to Mrs. Hughes. It was like talking to his Grandma Mildred. It was much easier to share his problems with Grandma Mildred than his parents because his grandma would never punish him or judge him. She was just there to love him and make him feel better. Usually that included a bowl of ice cream.

After hearing Mikey's story, Mrs. Hughes said, "Well, I don't blame Justin. If I were him, I might have felt angry that you hogged all the credit. I don't think Justin trusts you anymore. If you want to stay friends, you're going to have to earn back his trust."

Mrs. Hughes' advice was more like a spoonful of slimy medicine than a bowl of ice cream. Mikey also realized that she was right.

"Thanks, Mrs. Hughes. I'll try."

"I know you will. But now to the real reason I came to

see you. I can't find my car keys anywhere. Could you help me look for them?"

"You mean the keys that are in your hand?"

Mrs. Hughes opened her gloved palm and flinched in shock, seeing the keys there.

"That's them! My hand is always the last place I look. I guess it should be the first."

24

At 10:00 p.m. that Monday night, Mikey stood outside Justin's large house throwing pebbles at his second-story window.

Justin popped his head out of the window and whispered loudly, "What are you doing here, Mikey? You woke me up!"

"I know," Mikey whisper-shouted back, not wanting to alert Justin's parents. "Come down here so we can talk."

"No!" Justin whispered angrily. "I'm still mad at you. Go away!"

"I have to show you something. I'll stand out here all night if I have to!"

Justin rubbed his eyes and yawned. "Fine, but this won't change anything."

Justin came down, still dressed in his pajamas. Mikey stood next to his bike and signaled him over.

"What's so important?" asked Justin.

"Get your shoes on and ride your bike to the end of the block."

Mikey knew Justin wouldn't be able to contain his curiosity. Justin put on his warm clothes and sneakers and rode his bike to the end of the block where Mikey was waiting for him.

"Follow me," said Mikey, taking off down the block on his bike.

Justin followed after him, pedaling as hard as he could to keep up. Eventually, they ended up at the school.

Mikey marveled at what a different place the school

was at night when it was dark and deserted. Justin followed Mikey to the front entrance, where Mikey pulled out the big ring of keys that Principal Walker had left for him.

Then a loud voice shouted at them, "Hold it right there!" A bright flashlight shined in their faces.

It was Bill the security guard. He was a big guy and the chocolate all over his lips indicated he had been enjoying a late-night snack.

"What do you two think you're doing?" Bill bellowed, approaching fast. When he got close enough to make out their faces, he recognized Mikey.

"Oh, it's you, Principal. Sorry, I couldn't tell from over there."

"It's okay, Bill," said Mikey. "You did a good job."

"Really? Thank you, Principal! You know, it gets awful boring being the night watchman. Would it be okay if I listened to my radio? Principal Walker said I couldn't, but you understand, right?"

"Sure," said Mikey. "Go ahead."

"Thank you! Have a good night, sirs!"

"You too."

Bill puttered away, whistling a happy tune to himself.

Mikey opened the front door and ran down the hallway then out the back entrance of the school. Mikey turned and saw Justin looking fatigued but pressed onward.

"Mikey, this had better be good, or I'm never speaking to you again!"

Mikey stopped at the gym and pulled out another key to open the entry door. He stepped inside and flipped the switches, lighting up the great basketball gym in all its shimmering glory. Underneath the hoop was a bin full of basketballs.

"Wanna play?" asked Mikey with a devilish grin on his face.

"Uhhh ... yeah!" replied Justin.

The two had dreamed of playing on the gym basketball court their whole time at Prairie View. They were never good enough to be on the basketball team, and the big kids never let them join during recess.

Shooting the balls at hoops with a clear glass backboard, dribbling on a polished floor that squeaked against their shoes, was the most fun they'd ever had. Though it was only a school gym, it may as well have been New York's Madison Square Garden.

The boys had a three-point shooting contest and counted how many threes they could sink in sixty seconds. While one of them shot, the other timed and mimicked the sounds of a cheering crowd. Justin claimed victory by making one three-pointer next to Mikey's count of zero.

They played three games of H-O-R-S-E. Mikey took two of the three games with a dramatic backwards free throw over his head.

It was the first time all week that the boys had forgotten about the worries of running the school. They finally had the chance to just be kids again and neither wanted the night to end.

They wrapped up with a game of one-on-one. They were evenly matched as Justin was taller, but Mikey was faster. Neither one could shoot very well, but they played tough defense. After a few minutes they stopped keeping score since it was not about winning, just having fun.

After the game, the boys were drained. They collapsed on their backs at the center court line and tried to catch their breath.

"Listen," said Mikey. "I want you to know that you were right about everything you said. When I got caught up in the excitement, I did want to hog all the credit. I was a big jerk. I'm sorry."

"How big a jerk were you?" asked Justin, playfully.

"As big as the black hole in the center of the galaxy."

Justin laughed.

"You may be a big jerk, but you're an even *bigger* nerd!" Justin made himself laugh even harder.

"Shut up! I'm not nearly as big a nerd as *you*! Which one of us cried when he didn't get the gold ribbon at the science fair?"

"Hey! My tomato sauce volcano would have won if it didn't spew marinara all over the judge's shirt!"

The boys joked again as if they had never fought.

"So," said Mikey, "if I promise not to mess up again, will you come back to work with me?"

"Um, don't you think it's a little late for that? You're probably going to get fired on Monday."

"Maybe. But I don't want to go down without a fight. Are you with me?"

Mikey extended his hand.

Justin thought for a moment, then grabbed his hand and shook it vigorously.

"I'm always ready for a battle, good friend."

"Awesome. I have something for you," said Mikey. "Wait here."

Mikey brought over his backpack and pulled out a brand new badge. Unlike the last one, this one didn't look like he had thrown it together in five minutes. He had clearly put his time into cutting out a perfect star from construction paper, then made the effort to glue every inch of it with gold glitter.

Instead of "S.C." for Señor Consultant, the badge was inscribed with the words "Co-Principal."

"Do you accept your new position as co-principal?"

Justin was choked up, but managed to squeak, "Yes," as he took the badge from Mikey and pinned it on his shirt.

"So, Mr. Co-Principal," said Mikey, "any ideas on how we can keep our jobs?"

"It's just like winning at basketball," replied Justin. "We have to have a good defense."

25

Tuesday

Mikey and Justin stayed up all night preparing for the School Board's decision. If the board decided to fire them, they had an intricate last-ditch defense established. Justin had even borrowed his father's law books and found precedent for kids who were declared legally able to run companies when they received them as an inheritance. Why should a school be any different?

"Heck," said Justin closing a history text, "just a hundred years ago, a kid emperor named Puyi was running the entire nation of China!"

The friends rode their bikes to school together. They arrived at 7:30 a.m. to get everything in order and make sure the school was ready for the School Board's arrival.

Vice Principal Sherman met them at the door. As always, his short brown hair didn't have a strand out of place. He was wearing his signature dark brown suit, but for the first time, he wasn't wearing a tie.

"Principal McKenzie, Mr. Gluck, we have a—"

"It's Co-Principal McKenzie and Co-Principal Gluck now," Mikey corrected him.

"Yes, sirs. We have a problem. Follow me."

"What's going on?" asked Mikey, keeping up behind the fast-walking Mr. Sherman. "Is the School Board already here?"

"No. They called this morning and said they will arrive at 11:00 a.m. They requested a conference room. I recommend the library."

"No," said Justin. "Change it to the gym and assemble all the students. Whatever they have to say to us, they will have to say in front of the entire student body."

Mikey smiled at Justin's idea. "I agree," said Mikey. "If they fire us, maybe the sound of a thousand boos will change their minds."

"Yes, Co-Principals. I will make the arrangements. But that's not the problem. *This* is the problem."

Mr. Sherman pointed at the principal's office.

It was a disaster zone.

Someone had broken in and completely trashed the place. The computer was on the floor, smashed to pieces. Books were thrown off the shelves. Papers were strewn everywhere and torn to shreds. Rotten eggs were smattered against the walls and on the desk.

But worst of all, spray-painted in large red letters across the entire side of the wall were the words: *Principal Mikey Stinks!*

Mikey and Justin were frozen in shock. It smelled so awful, they couldn't stand near the door.

"Why would somebody do this?" Mikey asked.

"Well," said Justin, "I guess everyone is nice to the principal's face, but who knows what they are actually thinking behind our backs?"

"Have you heard anything?" Mikey snapped at Justin. "Did someone say something bad about me?"

"Look, Mikey. When it seemed like you and I weren't friends anymore, people did say some things to me, but nothing about this. Not everyone liked your anti-bullying rules. That's for sure."

"I thought so. This is one of the bully's last-ditch efforts to intimidate me. Well, we can't let them. When we find out who did it, he is getting expelled."

"Boys," Mr. Sherman interrupted. "as it happens, I *do* know who did it. But I'm warning you, this may be hard for you to see."

Mikey and Justin entered the vice principal's office. Mr. Sherman usually kept to himself inside and never let anybody in. When he was out, he always locked the door.

Mikey had never actually seen the inside of it and now he knew why. Mounted to the wall were two large TV screens. They must have been fifty inches each. On each screen were dozens more tiny screens showing different areas of the entire school.

Mr. Sherman explained, "When I got hired for the job, the first thing I did was install hidden surveillance cameras all over the school out of my own pocket. I made sure every inch of the school was covered so nobody would ever be able to get away with anything. It's the secret of my success."

Well, thought Mikey, that certainly explains Mr. Sherman's uncanny ability to be at the spot whenever anyone misbehaves.

Mr. Sherman continued, "As you might guess, I had the principal's office covered as well. I reviewed the recording. Principal, you aren't going to like what you see."

Mr. Sherman pressed a button on the remote. The screen showed a student entering the principal's office at 4:00 a.m. that morning wearing a hooded sweatshirt. The student removed the hood after entering the office, revealing her face.

Mikey's eyes widened and his jaw dropped.

"No," he murmured. "It can't be."

But the truth was undeniable. It was his sister, Tracy.

"The cameras caught her sneaking in through the school's kitchen window," Mr. Sherman explained. "She must have left it open for herself after doing her morning task. The security guard on duty was busy dancing to his radio and didn't see her."

Mikey and Justin looked at each other and grimaced.

All three continued to watch the horrific act of vandalism. She smashed the computer with a large rock. She threw the books all over the office. She spray-painted the disgusting message on the wall. "Principals, I need to know how you would like to proceed with this. If this is too much for you, Principal Mikey, I will talk to your sister for you."

"What will you do to her?"

"Whatever you say, Principal. But if it were up to me, I would have to say that this type of behavior more than calls for expulsion. But, I will do whatever you order me to do."

Mikey lowered his head, defeated. "You're right," he said. "This does warrant expulsion. But if it's going to happen, it should come from me."

26

As the students arrived to begin their Cool Points tasks, the rancid smell from the office wafted down the hallways. The school was abuzz with what had happened.

Justin suggested that nothing be cleaned up, as it was essentially a crime scene and evidence could get damaged.

Tracy did not come near the office all morning. Mikey didn't want to find her right away. He wanted to give her the chance to feel guilty enough to confess. That would go a long way and could definitely save her from getting expelled.

Justin and Mikey were supposed to be rehearsing their presentation in case the board decided to fire them. Mikey couldn't concentrate on that, though.

It was 10:30 a.m. Second recess had already ended and Tracy still hadn't confessed.

"Look," said Justin, "the school board could get here any minute. If you're going to talk to your sister while you're still principal, you better do it now."

"Okay," said Mikey. "Meet me in Mr. Sherman's office."

Tracy had also smashed the PA system, so Mikey had to walk to her classroom and pop his head in.

"Excuse me," said Mikey. "I need to speak with Tracy for a few minutes."

"O...okay," Tracy stammered.

Mikey saw Skyler and Katie look at one another and smirk. They were actually enjoying Tracy's nervousness.

"What ... what's going on, brother?" Tracy was trying to act calm, but not doing a good job.

"Tracy, do you have anything you want to tell me?"

"Um ... no. What's this about?"

"Just follow me."

Mikey and Tracy entered Mr. Sherman's office where the vice principal and Justin were waiting for them.

"Guys," said Mikey, "I'd like to speak with my sister alone, if you don't mind."

"Okay, we'll be right outside," said Justin. He and Mr. Sherman left the office and closed the door behind them.

"Tracy," said Mikey. "We know what you did."

"What did I do?"

Mikey sighed, upset that she was playing dumb right to his face. He picked up the remote and turned on the screen. It showed her in the middle of vandalizing the office.

"Oh no, oh no," said Tracy, quivering. "There are cameras?"

"Of course."

"Okay. Okay. I did it. But I had a good reason."

"Why? Do you really think I'm a bad principal?"

"No! You're great! Of course I didn't mean it. They said I had to."

"Skyler and Katie?"

"Yes! Plus all of their friends, too! Mikey, you don't understand what it's been like. When you started that anti-bullying rule, nobody would talk to me. Nobody! They wouldn't even stand close to me. They all thought I was your eyes and ears and would tell on them if they were the slightest bit mean to anybody. Do you know what it's like to not have a single person want to talk to you?"

Mikey felt awful. He had never considered what could happen to Tracy as a result of his anti-bullying policy. He really thought everyone would be happy not to be called names or picked on anymore. But all he did was create an atmosphere of fear where everyone was scared of being caught. That type of fear is the exact same feeling that a bully seeks to create in others. Mikey realized that he himself had become the school bully.

"I'm sorry," said Mikey. "I didn't consider that your friends might treat you differently."

"Of course not! You've only been thinking of yourself ever since you became principal! You didn't even acknowledge your best friend on television when they interviewed you. You created these stupid bully rules just so *you* wouldn't get bullied without Justin to defend you. You couldn't even see how unfair it was!"

"Maybe that's true," said Mikey. "But that still doesn't give you the right to vandalize school property. Why did you do it?"

"Because," said Tracy, "my friends said the only way to prove I was on their side and not yours was to trash your office and spray that message on the wall. I had to do it, or they wouldn't have spoken to me for the rest of the year. And you know what? This morning, everyone was friends with me again. Can't I just say I'm sorry and we'll forget about this?"

"No. It's not good," said Mikey. "All you've done is given in to peer pressure from girls you shouldn't be friends with. They don't have your best interests at heart. If I let you get away with this, you could continue listening to the wrong people for the rest of your life, getting into worse and worse trouble."

"Fine. You know what? Give me a detention or a day's suspension. Whatever."

"No, Tracy. I think ... I think I have to expel you."

"You wouldn't!"

"The girls at this school are a bad influence. Maybe you're better off at home."

"No, no, no. I am *not* getting expelled by my own brother. We love each other. You're supposed to look out for me."

"But … I really feel that I am."

"That's it. Call Mom and Dad right now. Let's see what they have to say."

"You really want me to get Mom and Dad involved? I think they would agree with me to get you away from these so-called friends of yours who have turned you into a thief, a liar and a vandal."

Tracy broke down crying. "Please, Mikey, you can't. You just … can't. I love you."

Mikey wasn't sure if the tears were a tactic to make him feel bad or if they were real. Maybe both. It didn't matter, though. Mikey saw no other option.

"I'm sorry, sis. I love you, too. But … you're ex—"

There was an abrupt knock at the door. Justin popped his head in.

"Mikey! The board members are here! We need to get everyone to the gym quick."

"Well," said Mikey to Tracy. "We have to go to the gym now. If I'm still principal when this is done, my decision stands. If not, the next principal can decide."

27

The time for judgment was at hand.

Mr. Sherman did a great job setting up the gym. Every student in the school was seated in the bleachers. A podium stood in the middle of the gym facing the students. The twelve members of the School Board plus Superintendent Matthews sat to the right of the podium at a long conference table. On the other side was an equally long table where the entire faculty sat.

Mikey and Justin sat next to one another in small chairs behind the podium. They each wore freshly ironed suits and ties.

Mikey could taste the tension in the air.

Superintendent Matthews was the first to take the podium. He wore the same gray suit and patted the sparse gray hairs on the sides of his bald head before speaking into the microphone.

"Greetings, students of Prairie View School. I am Superintendent Matthews. While we intended this to be a private conference, Vice Principal Sherman informed me that they preferred a public hearing. That's why you've been dragged out of class."

"It's okay! We don't mind!" shouted Stanley Roberts from the crowd.

"Right, well, here's how this is going to work. I will be the first to make a recommendation to the School Board based on my observations. After that, should any faculty member or the principal himself wish to present an opposing view, you will have the opportunity to make your argument. Then, all thirteen members of the board will vote as to whether to allow Mr. McKenzie to continue as principal or relieve him of his duties. A majority decision will carry."

Superintendent Matthews cleared his throat and took a sip of water.

"Ahem. After conducting a thorough inspection of the school's daily regiment under Principal McKenzie, it is my belief that he must be removed immediately."

There was a smatter of boos from the audience. Even though Mikey's new policies weren't as popular, the students didn't seem to like one of their own put on trial by an adult. Superintendent Matthews ignored them and continued.

"While many of his programs have proven successful in the short-term, most were ill-advised. For instance, the program known as the 'Cool Points' system is no different than common bribery. In addition, he has done away with homework, which was a very poor decision considering the school's low GAT scores. He also decreed that pizza be served every day and extended the lunch and P.E. periods by fifteen minutes each—minutes that could have been put toward math or science considering the lost time due to the morning tasks and extra recess. Oh, and need I even mention that his first day on the job he installed a makeshift go-kart track, a dangerous Slip 'N Slide, and a lice-infested petting zoo. In conclusion, Principal McKenzie, though his intentions may have been noble, is merely a child. He has run the school exactly as one would expect a child to run a school. To keep him in a position of power would be unsafe, irresponsible, and unfair to the students of the school who need a principal to guide them into adulthood, not bind them to their childhood. Lastly, because of her poor judgment, the board must also dismiss Principal Tabitha Walker to prevent such actions from occurring in the future. Thank you."

As Superintendent Matthews took his seat, the boos grew even louder. Everyone liked Principal Walker and hated the idea of losing not only Mikey, but her as well.

Vice Principal Sherman stood up and walked to the podium. Mikey was sure he would agree wholeheartedly with the superintendent. It would be almost impossible for Mikey to win with two recommendations going against him.

Mr. Sherman began, "Members of the board, students, and faculty, as most of you know I am Vice Principal Carl Sherman. I have been asked by the faculty to speak on their behalf and also to state my own opinion, which happens to be one and the same. After working with Principal McKenzie all week, it is my belief that Principal McKenzie absolutely must *remain* as principal of Prairie View School."

There was a gasp of shock from the audience.

Mr. Sherman continued, "I cannot emphasize enough how strongly I *disagree* with everything Superintendent Matthews said. He calls the Cool Points system bribery. But would you call it bribery that we reward students who perform well on a test with a good grade? Would you call it bribery that teachers get paid as a reward for performing our jobs? Of course not. Mikey simply saw that students are better motivated with greater incentives. The Cool Points are something tangible that good behavior and good work can be rewarded with. In my opinion, it seems to work far better than an abstract promise of a better future years down the line.

"The teachers have asked me to report to you that in this brief week, class participation has skyrocketed, test scores are up an average of a full letter grade, detentions are down by over seventy-five percent, and the overall reflection of the school is that the students are much happier and more enthusiastic about being here. Now, if you were given these results and the principal was anyone other than a ten-year-old kid, not only would you be offering him a raise, you would probably be making him superintendent of the school system!"

The crowd of students erupted in cheers.

"As for myself, I am a man who was raised in military schools and went on to serve in the United States Marine Corps. I was taught that tough love and tougher discipline are the best ways to run an outfit. But after this week, I've learned that there is another way. I've learned that you can inspire children to be their best simply by being their friend and listening to them. I used to spend my days handing out countless detentions, but if my system was working at all, I shouldn't have had to hand out nearly so many. Mikey came in, and suddenly, not only did kids want to do the right thing, they demanded the same of their peers.

"I say we aren't here to guide kids into adulthood. Adulthood will come no matter what. We're here to guide kids *through their childhood*. Mikey reminded us that you don't have to grow up in order to achieve greatness. Mikey showed us that each and every one of you in the audience can accomplish great things right here and now, if only us meddling adults didn't constantly stand in your way.

"In my unit, it didn't matter your race, age, creed, or color. Our leaders were always the best man or woman for the job. Members of the School Board, if Mikey McKenzie were in my squad, he would be my choice for squad leader. Thank you."

The crowd cheered their hearts out as Mr. Sherman took his seat with the faculty.

Superintendent Matthews returned to the podium. "Thank you, Mr. Sherman. Thanks ... a lot. Principal McKenzie, you are free to speak."

During Mr. Sherman's speech, Mikey and Justin had been frantically whispering to one another. They seemed to have come to an agreement.

Mikey stood up and walked toward the podium. He expected Justin to join him, but Justin stayed planted in his seat. He was shaking with nerves. Mikey urged him to get up, but he shook his head.

Exasperated, Mikey refused to let Justin sit this one out. He grabbed Justin by the arm and yanked him up to the podium next to him. He took a deep breath and began to speak.

"Members of the board, students, teachers ... what's up? You've been calling me Principal McKenzie all week, but that's not quite accurate. You should have been calling me Co-Principal McKenzie, because none of the changes would have been possible without my best friend, Co-Principal Justin Gluck. Let's hear it for Justin!"

As the crowd cheered for Justin, he smiled bigger than Mikey had ever seen him smile before. It was the first time he had ever been recognized by his schoolmates. He could hardly contain his joy.

Mikey continued, "As I once learned, one of the marks of a good leader is to be able to admit when he's made a mistake. I've come to realize that my anti-bullying policy was a very big mistake. We should treat one another with kindness and respect because it's the right thing to do, not because you're afraid of getting suspended. I am hereby striking down that policy. The consequences for bullying should be determined on a case-by-case basis by our head of discipline, Mr. Sherman."

The audience cheered.

"Lastly, I have had a discussion with my co-principal, and we have come to a decision. We are hereby resigning as co-principals of the school."

There was a collective gasp from the students and faculty.

Stanley shouted from the crowd, "No, dude! You can't!"

"To be honest," said Mikey, "one of the reasons I took the job was so that mean Mr. Sherman wouldn't be in charge, but after getting to know him, I think he would make a great principal. Please know that I very much enjoyed my time serving you, but when it comes down to it, the superintendent is right about a couple things. I'm just a kid. I want to enjoy being a kid while I still have the chance. Being an adult really isn't all it's cracked up to be. Even though I wasn't the most popular kid before this all happened, I miss being among you. I miss going to class. Strangely enough, I even miss trying to get my glasses back when you play 'keep away' with them. And most of all, I miss being on your side. We kids need to stick together. It's been an honor, but I quit. And I would like to officially resume my position as school nerd."

Justin approached the microphone and said simply, "Me too."

As Mikey left the podium there was stunned silence. Then, Mrs. Hughes stood up and began clapping. Then, all the teachers stood up and followed her lead. After the teachers, every student in the gym stood up and clapped for five minutes straight.

As Mikey and Justin basked in the applause, they looked at one another and wanted to cry, but they held their emotions in check. Now that they were normal kids again, that's the sort of thing that they could get teased about for years.

The superintendent approached the podium and tried to calm things down, but nobody listened to him. When it was quiet enough to speak, the superintendent pronounced, "Well, I guess we won't have to vote on whether or not to dismiss Principal Mikey, but there's still the matter of the absent Principal Walker. Who here votes to remove Principal Tabitha Walker from her position as principal?"

The vote was eight to five in favor of dismissal.

Principal Walker was fired. She didn't even get a chance to plead her case.

"The motion carries," said Superintendent Matthews. "By the rules of the county, Vice Principal Carl Sherman is hereby appointed as principal of Prairie View School. Meeting adjourned. Vice Principal, you may address your students."

Vice Principal Sherman approached the podium and looked out to the sea of children he was now in charge of. It was the moment he had waited for all his life. He could only think of one thing to say:

"No more homework!" Mr. Sherman declared, sending the crowd into a frenzy of cheers.

Vice Principal Sherman was laughing like crazy, then said, "Ahhh, I'm just kidding. You're totally going to have to start doing homework again. Gotcha!"

Mikey and Justin broke into laughter. As Mr. Sherman turned around and flashed a smile at them, they knew he was going to be a very tough, but also, a very good principal.

28

Following the assembly, Mikey, Justin and Mr. Sherman went back to their offices. Mikey was packing the few belongings that his sister hadn't destroyed.

Mr. Sherman came into the office and said, "Mikey, you have a call."

Mikey picked up the phone in Mr. Sherman's office.

"Hello, Mikey. Can you guess who this is?"

"Hi, Principal Walker."

"Please, you can call me Tabitha now. I wanted to tell you how proud I am of you. Mr. Sherman spoke very highly of your deeds. He assured me that he would be keeping all of your new changes in place."

"Thanks. I'm sorry about what happened to you, though. I feel like it's my fault."

"Don't be silly. It was my decision. Besides, it gives me more time to spend with my mother. Maybe I wasn't cut out to be a principal like you are. I think I'll go back to what I really love. Teaching."

"I think you'd be a great teacher."

"Thank you, Mikey. I look forward to keeping track of your sure-to-be-exciting life."

Just before lunch, Principal Sherman called Mikey and Tracy into his office.

As they sat outside, Tracy was still furious at Mikey and refused to even look at him. She looked like she hadn't stopped crying since their meeting.

Mikey had never felt worse in his life. At that moment,

a crushing realization swept over him. Despite all that happened, he loved his sister more than anyone else in the world. As such, it was his job to do everything in his power to make her happy.

He secretly commenced *Operation Save Your Sister*.

"Mikey, Tracy, please come in," said Principal Sherman.

Mikey and Tracy took their seats in front of Principal Sherman's desk.

"Well," he said. "I hate for this to be one of my first acts as principal, but the evidence is overwhelming. Tracy McKenzie, the video evidence shows you destroying the principal's office along with thousands of dollars in property. Since it's your second major infraction in two weeks, I see no other choice but to expel you from school."

"No!" said Mikey. "She's innocent!"

"What?" said Principal Sherman.

Tracy was equally surprised.

"The only reason Tracy wrecked the office is because … I ordered her to. I thought if the office were to get trashed, then I could blame some of the school's worst trouble-makers and expel them. I would have done it myself, but I was afraid of getting caught by the security guard. So, not knowing about the cameras, I ordered Tracy to do it, under threat that I would reverse my decision and have her expelled again. You see, it was really all my fault."

"Is that true, Tracy?" inquired Principal Sherman.

Tracy looked at Mikey, saying 'thank you' as hard as she could with her eyes, then nodded to Principal Sherman.

Principal Sherman leaned back and sighed. He didn't seem sure about whether he believed Mikey's story or not, but came to a decision.

"Well, Mikey," said Principal Sherman, "this is a very serious offense. I was going to hand you your paycheck for the week, but now it's going to have to go toward replacement of the office supplies. Not only are you responsible for this vandalism, you were planning to frame an innocent student. *But* … I suppose we can let you off with … a week's suspension. And Ms. McKenzie, I know a little something about following orders, so you are not expelled. You are also suspended for the rest of the week. Plus I expect both of you to clean this office until it's spotless by lunchtime. Dismissed."

Mikey and Tracy left the office and breathed a giant sigh of relief. Tracy's classmates populated the hallway, but she didn't care anymore. In front of everyone, she gave Mikey the biggest hug of his life.

Tracy and Mikey actually enjoyed their week off school together. They played videogames and went on several nature hikes.

Mikey was even able to connect to Principal Walker's Class Cam for both his and Tracy's classrooms, so they never missed a single class.

Principal Sherman was good to his word and kept all of Mikey's changes in place.

The Cool Points system continued to work well and the students continued to earn their best grades ever thanks to all the extra credit opportunities.

Tracy stopped hanging out with Skyler and Katie. Instead, she made new friends who liked her for who she was. She may not have been as popular, but she was happier than she'd ever been.

A few months later, when the school received its results on the GATs, the scores were so high that Prairie View was awarded the most funding in its history. As a tribute to Mikey and Justin's efforts, Principal Sherman put the funds toward a brand new computer lab filled with top-of-the-line systems.

Mr. Sherman named it: The McKenzie-Gluck Computer Lab.

At the end of the year, when the students finished their physical fitness tests, they were happy to report that the school was now perfectly average. No longer were they the least athletic school in the state.

But that's getting way ahead of things.

The best moment for Mikey came a month after he had quit as principal. He had gone to the eye doctor and found out his vision had improved enough that he could be issued standard athletic goggles.

Wearing the goggles on the soccer field made him feel like a new man. No longer worried about the twenty-one lenses getting smashed, he played like a maniac. He even made the game-winning save that won his team the championship. The team dog-piled him in celebration.

Seeing Justin cheer for him on the sidelines, he thought it might be the best moment of his life. Afterward, the whole team went out for pizza, but Mikey couldn't bite a single slice as he had grown super sick of it.

Looking back, Mikey laughed at the days when all he wanted was for adults to take him seriously. After spending a week as the principal of his school, he kind of liked the idea of not being taken so seriously anymore. After all, he was still just a kid.

And no kid should take himself too seriously.

Sometime that spring, Mikey walked to the corner of Walnut and Pine to check on his squirrel suspension bridge.

A sign had been posted that said: *Watch for falling squirrels*.

Thus began: Operation Squirrel Parachutes.

Quick! While the principal is sleeping, check out <u>DerekTaylorKent.com</u> for more of my awesome books, like the spooky and popular Scary School series!

You can even write to me at <u>Derek@DerekTaylorKent.com</u> with any questions or to request a school visit! I even do video-feed Skype visits all over the world! Hope to see you soon!

Derek Taylor Kent

is an author, screenwriter, and performer based out of Los Angeles, California. His is best known for his award-winning middle-grade series *Scary School*, published by HarperCollins. Picture books include the #1 best-selling *El Perro con Sombrero, Simon and the Solar System,* and *Counting Sea Life with the Little Seahorse,* which was co-authored with his wife, best-selling children's author Sheri Fink. His first novel for grown ups, *Kubrick's Game,* was published in 2016 and became a #1 best-selling thriller and won the Reader's Favorite award for best fiction audiobook of 2017, narrated by Jonathan Frakes and Yvette Nicole Brown. In his spare time, Derek loves coaching basketball, cooking pasta, and playing with his Italian Greyhound, Zander. You can learn more about Derek and his books at www.DerekTaylorKent.com and www.ScarySchool.com. You can also check out Sheri's books at www.SheriFink.com.

Paul
Louis
Smith

    was born in Portland, Oregon, and grew up loving to draw. Despite years of teachers telling him not to doodle in class, he never stopped and still loves to draw. He now makes his own cartoons and illustrates for comics, animations, and of course, Derek Taylor Kent. You can find more of his work on the YouTube channel MapleSistersMedia, CollegeHumor.com, and Paul-louis-smith.tumblr.com

PRINCIPAL MIKEY